AFTER EMMA

AFTER EMMA

by

SHEILA HOCKEN

LONDON
VICTOR GOLLANCZ LTD
1988

This book is dedicated to Betty Glenn, who has proved to be a friend in deed, and Moira Shaw for typing all my manuscripts to perfection.

First published in Great Britain 1988
by Victor Gollancz Ltd,
14 Henrietta Street, London WC2E 8QJ

Published by arrangement with Sphere Books Ltd

British Library Cataloguing in Publication Data
Hocken, Sheila
After Emma.
1. Guide dogs — Biography   2. Labrador
retriever — Biography
I. Title
636.7'52   HV1780.S4
ISBN 0–575–04255–9

Typeset at The Spartan Press Limited,
Lymington, Hants
and printed in Great Britain by
St Edmundsbury Press Ltd, Bury St Edmunds, Suffolk
Illustrations originated and printed by
Thomas Campone, Southampton

CONTENTS

ILLUSTRATIONS

FOREWORD

I was born in Beeston, Nottingham, in 1946, into a family where disability was the norm. My mum, dad and elder brother, Graham, have eye defects. My mum has two disabilities to contend with: she has very badly impaired hearing as well. I did not escape the congenital hereditary cataracts.

You would imagine that life in such a family would be very difficult. It was for my parents, but my brother and I were unaware of that as children. Only now, in retrospect, do I realize how much my parents struggled and sacrificed to bring myself and my brother up as normally as possible. They fought tooth and nail to keep us children at home when the education authorities tried to insist that we be sent away to a special school for blind children.

Both my parents had been deprived of a loving family life. My father had been sent away to school from a very early age and my mother had been orphaned. I thank my lucky stars that they won their fight and we were accepted by a normal sighted school. I admit that life was a struggle, but it's far better to struggle as a child than be thrown out into the world after a sheltered early life.

I learnt to accept the knocks and bangs, both mental and physical. I remember, when I was about seven years old, my best friend at school had unscarred legs. Mine were always covered in cuts and bruises, and I usually had a lump on the forehead as well. I asked her how she managed not to fall over. She just laughed at me, thinking I was clumsy. It was from then on I began to realize that I had very poor sight and the rest of the world could avoid walking into lamp-posts and falling up kerbs.

I admit that I would have had a far better education, as far as the three Rs are concerned, if I'd have been sent away to a special school, but I managed to cope with my school work by going up to look at the blackboard and asking people to read small print in the school books for me. I was able to see most things if I could get close enough, and by that I mean sometimes my nose would get in the way.

Even as a child, I sought out the advantages of my situation. I remember going to special Christmas parties for blind children and we always received a Christmas present from the Royal National Institute for the Blind. We benefited from holidays, too, when my parents could afford it. There were special boarding houses available at cheap rates to visually impaired families. I remember spending a week at one of them, one of the happiest weeks of my childhood, and it was there I met totally blind people for the first time.

I felt desperately sorry for them, and yet it was wonderful to have a little sight in a blind world. I remember the glee I felt at helping them with simple tasks like taking them to the door, or telling them what colour dress they were wearing, for, at that time, although my vision was very poor, I had colour perception. I was unable to distinguish patterns or vague colours like creams and greys and fawns, but I could see bright reds and greens and blues.

School was comparatively easy compared to my later years and teens, when I had to find a job and get myself to and from work. I was very lucky and found a job as a telephonist, even though it meant me catching two buses to get to work. I tried to live a normal teenage existence, but it never worked out. My friends wore make-up and high-heeled shoes. No-one had ever shown me how to put make-up on and I daren't wear heels. It was hard enough walking in flat shoes. They had boyfriends and dates, dances on a Friday night and trips to the pictures. Well, admittedly, going to the cinema wouldn't have done much for me but I could have pretended to see the film. I had become very good at pretending to see things when I really couldn't, to try and be in with the crowd.

I, for one, never long to return to being a teenager. It was a terrible time for me. I always yearned to be independent, just to prove that I was as good as everyone else, and when I had the opportunity to share a flat with a friend, I took it, eagerly. I had a good job and a flat but I still wasn't mobile, not in the strict sense of the word. I was able to fight my way to work and back every day — and fight it was. My own fault: I refused to carry a white stick. I felt ashamed of being blind and I didn't want to ask people for help. I marvel now that I'm still here. I should have been run over.

And then Emma changed everything.

I was told by a social worker that I could apply for a guide dog. I didn't hesitate. I'd always loved dogs. My first recollections are of wanting one. As a child, I had to make do with borrowing other people's — any dog would do, just so long as I could take it for a walk. Even at the age of nine, I wanted to train dogs. There was a little black and white mongrel that lived round the corner from us, belonging to an old lady, and I went every evening after school to teach that little dog to retrieve a rubber bone.

I was accepted as a candidate for guide-dog training and went to the Leamington Spa Training Centre in July 1966, and it was there I met Emma, a chocolate-coloured Labrador.

She changed everything so completely that life before Emma seems like a nightmare now. With Emma to guide me, the world was my oyster. I could go anywhere I chose, any time I wanted. She was always willing and eager to take me.

The partnership we had bears no relationship to that of an ordinary pet dog and owner. We were as one. I had six legs with a chocolate bit down one side. We conquered my blind world together, Emma and I. The friend who we were sharing a flat with had to move from Nottingham because of her job. That didn't bother us. We were quite happy to live on our own. Emma was the start of my good fortune for, without her, I would never have met my husband, Don.

We met at Radio Nottingham's first Open Day, though we had spoken on the telephone before that. I had been involved in programmes for the blind, produced by George Miller, a blind journalist. That particular day, George had brought a friend with him. A friend who had a voice like deep brown velvet and I fell for it, hook, line and sinker. I was in love.

Life has never been a bed of roses but someone told me, a long time ago, that I was the sort of person who could fall in a cesspit and come out smelling of violets. Well, I have to admit, she was right! George's friend with the velvet voice was Don, but he was married and I was blind. No man would ever want me — I was so convinced of that. What I didn't realize was that Don's marriage had broken down. He and his wife were only living together for the sake of their daughter, Susan, and, more importantly, he fell in love with me.

I had to wait five years before Don was free. It was Emma who kept me sane through the lonely, dark nights and long years of waiting for the man I loved. He was worth waiting for. Don and I were married and I felt totally contented. I had everything anyone could possibly wish for in life, but there was more to come in my string of good fortune.

My father, my brother Graham and myself had all had eye

operations. They'd never been successful, and all our relatives had suffered the same fate. Naturally, we had given up the hope of ever being able to see. By this time, at the age of twenty-nine, the little sight I'd had as a child had diminished very slowly over the years, leaving me only with perception of light and dark. Graham had a little more vision and had sought information regarding a new type of soft contact lens available. The contact lens specialist he'd visited had recommended Graham to see an eye surgeon. New developments in micro-surgery could mean hope.

We both went to see the eye specialist. He was quite hopeful over my brother's sight prospects. Mine were a little different, he informed me, and he couldn't hold out much hope for sight but he offered to try. As this was a new technique and my brother only had one eye, it was decided that I should be the guinea pig. After all, I had nothing to lose.

I went for the operation in September 1975. It was successful, beyond all our wildest dreams. I say "our" and not "my" because everyone seemed to be involved. The eye surgeon, I think, was more surprised than anyone at the amount and the value of sight I had obtained. I had, literally, the time of my life seeing everything. Clouds and sunsets, raindrops and waves, birds and sheep, rainbows and frost on slate roofs. I have had sight for twelve years and never will I take it for granted. If I live to three hundred, I will still open my eyes in the morning and look out and think how beautiful and green my grass is.

Emma was then eleven and was able to retire, to live the rest of her life as a pet dog. I took her out for walks. I watched her cantering through the woods, stopping to sniff at exciting scents under trees and round bushes.

When I became pregnant, both Don and I were delighted, but there was just one little black cloud on the horizon: would my baby be able to see? We knew that there was a 50-50 chance of blindness and, I must admit, at that point, I felt convinced that I'd had my share of miracles and couldn't expect any more in one lifetime. But my baby was a little girl — just what I wanted — and she had perfect sight. Life in the Hocken household was idyllic.

I then wrote my first book, *Emma and I*. I wanted to tell the world what a fabulous dog she was and how wonderful my life had been. I wanted them to understand the plight of blind people and the need for constructive help, rather than just sympathy, and I had a very unusual and wonderful story to tell.

When the book was published, my feet left the ground and didn't come down again for a long time. Emma and I, and Don, went on a nationwide publicity tour. Television stations, radio and newspapers — we visited them all the length and breadth of Britain. We even went to America, when the book was published over there. Sad to say, we only spent five days in New York. The American publishers wanted us to spend three weeks touring the States. It would have meant a great deal more money and success, as far as the book was concerned, but I couldn't leave Emma for that long. I would have refused the trip completely if it had not stated in the contract I'd signed that I agreed to visit the States. I turned down visits to Australia and France and many other countries because of Emma. She had looked after me for all those years. Now she was my responsibility and I had to look after her. I can't help wishing the opportunity would come my way again.

At the age of fourteen, Emma was joined by another chocolate Labrador, Buttons. She was a year old and unwanted, and I couldn't bear to think of an unwanted chocolate Labrador. It was my duty to take her in. She was rapidly followed by Bracken and Mocha, two more chocolate Labradors. The dog-mania had begun. Teak, a German shorthaired pointer, and Shadow, a black Labrador, joined us a year later.

On 29 November 1981, Emma died. She was seventeen. At fourteen years old, Emma could outwalk any of our Labradors. She always loved playing the retrieve games and would race past Buttons and Bracken to take hold of the toy first. At fifteen her age began to tell, as she was losing her sight and hearing, but this never detracted from her enjoyment of life. She lived her seventeen years to the full. Her death left a gaping hole inside me. Like losing an arm or a leg, it can never be replaced. Fortunately, I have hundreds of pictures of Emma and some beautiful paintings. I also have her on video tape. Six years have passed since Emma's death but I am still unable to watch her tapes, so I cherish them and I hope that one day, in the future, I will be able to view them without grief.

CHAPTER ONE

KATY

———————————

I stood in Mrs Walmsley's kitchen, sobbing uncontrollably.

"I'm sorry," I gasped between the sobs.

"Don't worry." Mrs Walmsley handed me a paper handkerchief. "I quite understand how you feel. It must be terrible losing a dog so young."

Only two weeks had passed since our beloved black Labrador, Shadow, had been put to sleep to save her any further suffering from bone cancer. She was only two years old and I shall always carry the fear and dread of those six months in which I struggled to save her life. My own local vet had operated and removed part of the damaged bone in Shadow's shoulder. This had failed and he advised me to seek more specialized advice. Although the lab report had come back with a positive diagnosis of bone cancer, he was still not convinced as this is a very rare disease to find in the shoulder blade of a dog. It appears more often in the long bones of the dog's legs. With this knowledge in mind, he advised me to take Shadow to the Royal Veterinary College in Hertfordshire. Hope battled with despair as I travelled the hundred or so miles to the college, praying every second of the journey that my vet was wrong and Shadow could be saved. The bone specialist at the college delivered the same verdict: There was nothing he, or anyone else, could do and I was advised to have Shadow put to sleep. The awesome responsibility, that I had to name the day Shadow would die, will remain with me forever.

I had come to Mrs Walmsley's home to buy another little black Labrador puppy, who, on first sight, so reminded me of Shadow as a puppy that I was unable to control my grief. I saw Betty, through my tears, sitting in the lounge with the shiny black puppy on her knee, talking to Mr Walmsley. Betty had shared my grief over Shadow and proved to be a tower of strength to me. Being unable to see enough to drive myself, Betty was always willing to drive the car for me, never once telling me it was inconvenient that I needed to take Shadow to the vet, or that it was too much effort to take me down to the college in Hertfordshire. Our friendship had been sealed for life when, two years previously, Betty had taken one of Buttons' puppies and, despite the fact that she had never owned a dog before in her life, she proved to be an exemplary owner. As soon as I mentioned to her the thought of finding another black Labrador, she had offered immediately to drive me anywhere, at any time. Not that Don, my husband, wouldn't have done the same, but he had a busy chiropody practice to run.

"Do you like her?" Betty asked me, as I walked through into the lounge, having wiped the last of my tears away.

"She's beautiful," I said.

She wasn't quite like Shadow. She did resemble her in size and length of head, but her ears were enormous, whereas Shadow's had been very neat and small. That was probably a good thing, as Katy (her chosen name) wouldn't remind me too much of Shadow.

On the way home, the puppy sat on my knee in the car, watching with eager interest everything that passed, her huge ears flicking backwards and forwards.

"Are you pleased with her?" Betty said.

"Yes," I said, unsure of my emotions. Deep inside, I had a

feeling that I'd betrayed my beloved Shadow. Here I was, only a fortnight later, taking another black Labrador home. I told myself that Katy wasn't a replacement but she would help to fill the gaping hole of grief. She wouldn't help me to forget Shadow — nothing would ever do that — although she would keep me occupied. Even the best behaved puppy is a handful and needs constant attention, and maybe little Katy would, in some way, help ease the burden of loss.

The dogs were waiting eagerly to greet the newcomer. I had no qualms whatsoever that any of them would be nasty. I could trust them implicitly with anything small and defenceless. Bracken wagged his tail furiously and nuzzled her gently with a warm welcome. Teak pushed her affectionately and poor little Katy was rolled on her back. Mocha danced round with great excitement, not quite knowing what to do, while Buttons ploughed in, pushing everyone else out of the way, determined that this was her puppy and she was to play mum. Our little Katy was welcomed by all. Don came rushing out of the surgery and scooped Katy up from under Buttons.

"Oh, she's beautiful," he said, as the little puppy nuzzled his tie, her whole body wriggling with tail-wag.

After the initial excitement, everyone settled into their regular routine. Teak raced up and down the garden. We had fenced the lawn part of our garden off, after realizing that five dogs and a lawn just don't go. The dogs had a large area, paved and gravelled for cleanliness. Only Teak could jump the fence onto the lawn and race to the back of the garden where the cats lived. Although my Siamese live outside, I must explain to you they have a cat house — a large house, six by eight foot, double glazed and fibreglass lined, with an oil-filled radiator, lighting, and a radio to keep them company — and a large run with grass and trees in it. I had decided, a couple of years back, that it was much safer to keep the cats in a large pen. We live on a main road and none of my Siamese has any sense of danger. Ming, the oldest and, one would assume, the wisest, has diced with death on many occasions. She has always held the false belief that nothing or no-one could possibly hurt her. I have had so many cats tragically killed on the roads that when I bought Ming, my first Siamese, I was determined not to let it happen again. So Ming, along with Rahni, Zimba and Holly, had never been allowed to roam freely.

I was finding it more and more difficult to keep the cats contained inside the house. Kerensa, my daughter, was growing up and could reach the back door-knob. Visitors were constantly coming and going and forgetting to close doors behind them. In fact, our home was beginning to resemble Paddington Station in the rush hour. It was after one of Ming's skirmishes that I decided something must be done. She has always managed to choose the worst possible occasion to escape and her last fracas was done in style. It was dark and snowy, five o'clock, the rush-hour traffic was making our house shake. Kerensa had been unable to resist opening the back door and, as she was standing gazing with childish delight at the falling snow, Ming had shot between her legs and, with the speed of a greyhound, raced down the drive onto the main road.

I found her, back arched, tail bushed, her ears lying back and a ferocious growl emitting from her usually sublime face. She was defying an articulated lorry to run her over. I decided it was time to provide the cats with a home and pen that would keep them safe for the rest of their lives.

Teak had been overjoyed at the new set up for the cats. It had supplied her active mind with something to do. She now spends most of her free time racing around the cat run. It is only her hunting instinct which keeps her going. She likes the cats and is quite friendly with them when I let her into their run to say hello, but she has to do something, so she might as well pretend to point and hunt the cats all day. I have never, ever seen Teak sit still. She's either fast asleep or racing somewhere, always busy, always rushing around. Even food time has to be a rushed affair. On the stroke of four, when food is dolled out, Teak is darting to the back door, giving it a nudge and tearing back down the garden again. It took her some months, after she first arrived, to realize that if she didn't eat all her dinner up in one go, instead of dashing back out into the garden to see what was happening, someone else would eat it.

I could watch Teak for hours as she canters gracefully up and down the garden. She reminds me of a young racehorse, raring to go. She takes the fence with the experience of a National winner. Many people mistake Teak for a Doberman. I suppose it's the docked tail and pointed nose. To me, she looks nothing like that breed. Her ears are much larger, with the texture of soft, new window leathers. She has a slender, feminine head, belied by the huge brown nose stuck on the end. She appears, at first glance, very lady-like and graceful but her eyes tell the truth — a warm, hazelnut brown, full of mischief. She is, basically, the same colour as the chocolate Labradors, although, by some strange quirk, the Kennel Club always refer to German shorthaired pointers' brown as "liver". I hate that, but then I can't abide liver. I much prefer to call her chocolate. I always cringed if anyone referred to Emma as a liver colour. But Teak also has speckles of silver along her paws, up her chest and round her muzzle.

Bracken had pottered off, like a gentleman, into the lounge and was fast asleep on the settee. I viewed him with envy. I had work to do. He stretched himself out, his head nestled on the cushion. When I switched the vacuum cleaner on, he opened one bleary eye, just to check.

"No, not today," I told him.

He lifted his head slightly and put those rose-petal ears on. He turns his ears back and curls them round into a rose-petal shape. It gives him a little boy lost look. Whenever he hears the vacuum cleaner switched on, he always checks to see if I have the small attachment on or not. The sight of that puts him into total ecstasy. He starts giving little low woofs and turns himself in circles, rolls on the floor and pads his feet in the air. He adores being vacuumed with the small attachment.

Once he'd checked it wasn't cleaning time for him, he stretched out a little further, gave a deep sigh and let his head fall back on the cushion. He's not a tall dog — about twenty inches at the shoulders — but he's all muscle, as solid as they come, with a broad masculine head and a thick, otter-like tail, all a true deep, rich, chocolate colour. His best assets are his eyes. They are a lovely soft gold, the colour of ripe pears.

When I returned to the kitchen to check what little Katy was up to, I saw Mocha and Buttons still sitting on either side of the gate like china dog models. Mocha had her eyes fixed on a brick to the left of her, staring intently at it. Over the years, I've come to the conclusion that there must be something wrong with Mocha. She's not "all there". A sweeter dog you could never wish to meet, ever friendly and pleasant. She never pulls on the lead. In the park, she follows behind, never running off. She always has a faraway look in her dark brown eyes, as if she's thinking of a better place somewhere. Sometimes she responds immediately to the call of her name, but most of the time she sits, her head tilted upwards, apparently engrossed and fascinated by things no one else can see.

I normally have to call her twice or even go over and give her a little prod to bring her back to earth, at which point she throws herself up and down on the spot. One could never pretend Mocha was feminine or delicate, though she does have a beautiful coat. It's soft and close-lying like neat-fitting satin, but her figure leaves a lot to be desired. She hangs underneath like a cow who wants milking and I've often thought of making her a pair of corsets. The problem is that she won't exercise herself, so she's grown flabby. She gets the same opportunities to run as all the other dogs, who gallop round the woods for an hour every morning. But Mocha plods. I've tried throwing a toy for her in the back garden, but she doesn't seem to notice it. On my command of "fetch", she leaps up and down in great excitement and then looks around her in bewilderment: what was it you wanted? Where is it? I can't see anything.

I take her along to the squeaky toy and point it out to her. "There you are, Mocha. That's what I want you to fetch."

At that point, she usually plonks her bottom on the grass, throws her nose up to the sky and goes into a daydream.

Buttons is bone idle. Most Labradors are. Probably that's why I'm attracted to them. I'm basically idle and I have a tendency to over-eat, just like them. I always think that the eyes can tell so much about a dog and Buttons is no exception. Her eyes are yellow and cold, almost evil. She's heavily built, like a hippopotamus, and stands quite a bit taller than Bracken. She has the same rich chocolate coat as Mocha and Bracken but hers tends to have a curl along the back. She's the show-standard Labrador among our flock and has won quite a few prizes in her breed classes. She used to enjoy going to shows but I became quite disillusioned and felt that winning a prize for how your dog looks doesn't really add up to much. It's what's inside that really matters and I'm sure Buttons' head is full of wicked thoughts.

She is forever on the scrounge, pleading malnutrition. One only has to look at her body to know how well fed she really is. When she heard me peeling the potatoes, she looked at me through the kitchen window, her very tiny little ears folding forwards and a big pink tongue licking her brown muzzle. Her yellow eyes sparkled for a moment in anticipation of food.

"It's nowhere near your dinner-time yet, Buttons, you'll have to wait."

She knew what I was talking about . . . her dinner. She lives and dies for dinner-time. She drew her ears back and gave me a disgusted look and flopped down on the path with a groan.

Watching and training a puppy is a twenty-four-hour occupation and I needed eyes in the back of my head. It had been two years since I last trained a puppy and I had forgotten how mischievous they can be. I was peeling the potatoes, scolding Buttons and trying to keep half an eye on Katy, when I spotted a large white teddy bear pushing his way through the kitchen door. I'd never seen any of Kerensa's teddy bears get up and go and it made me jump. I dropped the potato in the bowl and showered myself with scrapings and brown water. Then I saw the little black Labrador, her teeth firmly sunk into the back of its neck. She tried to shake it. The teddy bear, at least twenty times the size of Katy, refused to be shook and fell backwards, pinning her to the kitchen floor. Luckily, Kerensa wasn't around to see this. She's got quite protective over her furry toys, especially as so many of them have ended up shredded on the lawn.

I knew better than to shout at Katy. A little puppy doesn't realize teddy bears aren't to be shaken and killed and, after all, she'd struggled all the way downstairs and into the kitchen just to show me her prize. So I praised her, but told her the teddy wasn't for dogs and swopped it for a squeaky toy. She wasn't appeased. She fancied the teddy bear. She sat down and looked sad, a very easy expression for a little black Labrador puppy, for she appeared to have been given skin far too big for her. She looked like a Labrador in a Great Dane's coat and, as she sat, her nose pointing down to the floor, the rolls of skin gathered above her eyes and along her cheeks, and her huge ears flapped.

"I'm sorry, Katy. Kerensa would never forgive me if you ate her favourite teddy bear."

Her tiny black tail thumped on the kitchen floor and, as she looked at me, the skin rippled off her nose and forehead and ended up in large rolls just above her tail.

The one thing I hate about having a new puppy is the house-training. It's not so much the mess I mind cleaning up, but the vigilance needed to train a young puppy. Katy had been very clean on her first day with us but the night time I knew would be different. I spread newspapers liberally onto the dog room floor before I retired to bed. I was awakened the next morning at seven o'clock by small, but furious, barking. It was Katy. She had heard the newspaper boy come and, unlike the other dogs, was not accustomed to the strange noises of her new home. I jumped out of bed, hoping and praying that the dog room floor was clean. After the initial fanfare of tail-wags and joyous snuffles, the dogs rushed out into the garden. The dog room was spotless. I couldn't believe it. No damp patches. Nothing chewed. Was this just a one-off night or was Katy a paragon of virtue?

As Don and Kerensa entered the kitchen, I was still standing staring into the dog room in astonishment.

"What's the matter?" Don asked.

"Nothing," I told him.

"Was Katy all right in the night?"

"Yes, fine. Look at the dog room. There's nothing at all. No damage . . . no mess."

"Well, what are you worrying about?" Don smiled as he reached for the packet of cornflakes.

"It's too good to be true," I told him. "Puppies of Katy's age just can't stop themselves from doing naughty things."

Don chuckled. "Yes," he agreed. "I can remember Bracken at that age. Every time one of us blinked, he destroyed something."

Kerensa was dressed and tugging at my sleeve, asking if I was taking Katy out for a walk and if so could she come with me.

"Yes, of course," I said. "Daddy will take the others out this morning. I must start taking Katy out," I told Kerensa, "so that she gets socialized."

Kerensa was just five. "What does 'socialized' mean, Mummy?"

I tried to explain to her, as best I could, that Katy wasn't used to the outside world. Big lorries, roadworks and lots of people might frighten her and unless she got used to them while she was a little puppy, she'd grow up into a nervous dog. Kerensa was overjoyed as we walked down the drive, feeling that she was taking part in the new puppy's socialization.

"Where are we going to take her first, Mummy? Can we go to the shop. . . ? Then can we go on the fields. . . ? And then can we go. . . ?"

"Wait a minute, Kerensa," I said. "We can only do one thing at once. I think, just for this morning, we'll take her for a short walk round the block so that she gets used to traffic and we can teach her to sit at the kerb."

"Are you going to teach her the Green Cross Code?" Kerensa asked with delight. "I can tell her that, I've learnt all about it at school."

"I don't think Katy would understand that, but perhaps you can teach me."

I always try to remember that Kerensa is sharing her childhood with five dogs and it is important that she must be a part of it, having no other children to play with except when she goes to school.

At the bottom of the drive we approached the main road, which trembled with heavy lorries and large double-decker buses. Katy gave them an unperturbed glance. On reaching the first road, I gave Katy her first lesson in social behaviour:

sitting at kerbs. I was so intent on showing Katy how to sit correctly, crouching down beside her so she wouldn't be afraid, I forgot it had been raining heavily during the night. A lorry passed and I suddenly resembled a soggy Dalmation. Kerensa and, I'm convinced, Katy too, laughed at me.

The crowds of people and heavy traffic we met on our first walk were greeted by Katy as if she'd walked the pavements for years. She was far too interested in the autumn leaves that were blowing along the pavements in waves to be distracted by other sounds or sights. She jumped each flurry as it came towards her, snapping at the leaves with total joy. I stopped and picked up one or two of the leaves and threw them a little way for her. I did my best to ensure that her first walk would be one of enjoyment and not disasters.

I approached Katy's first training lesson that afternoon with trepidation. She was so full of potential, so keen to learn and eager to please and I was afraid of making mistakes. My first aim was to teach her to come to me immediately when called. But, at eleven weeks old, a puppy's capability of concentration is very limited and I knew, from bitter experience with Bracken, that the first thing I must do was ensure that Katy enjoyed her training sessions. I had always carried out Bracken's training with serious determination.

I took Katy onto the front lawn to do recalls. I felt there would be more things there to distract her. I waited until she was totally engrossed in a clump of Michaelmas daisies and then sat down on the lawn, threw a pair of old knotted tights up and down in the air, started laughing to myself, calling Katy. Katy, intrigued at my strange behaviour, left the Michaelmas daisies and came dashing over. The milkman was also intrigued. I don't know how long he'd been standing there on the drive watching me, but his, "Excuse me, m'duck!" made me jump out of my skin. How do you explain to the milkman that rolling on a wet front lawn with an old pair of tights is normal? I decided not to try. I just gave him his weekly dues and ignored the quizzical expression on his face.

CHAPTER TWO

ONE OVER THE EIGHT, KATE

I soon discovered that Katy wasn't quite as perfect as she'd first appeared. She had a thing about carrying bowls full of water around with her. I always kept two large, heavy bowls filled with water, one in the dog room, one under the bench in the kitchen and, suddenly, they were disappearing. I'd find them in all kinds of strange places. Under the chair in the lounge. In the back garden. A trail of water always leaving the telltale signs of movement of bowls. It didn't occur to me that it was Katy who was carrying them about. She was only the size of a bowl herself and couldn't possibly have the strength to lift one, or so I thought, until I actually saw her performing. She picked the bowl up and walked with it, trying to keep it the right way up and not spill any water. She wasn't terribly successful. They were so heavy, she had to keep putting them down and having a rest. As inconvenient as this little game of hers was, I was disinclined to prevent it. After all, she was a retriever and a water dog.

Labradors were originally bred to help the fishermen bring in the nets from the sea, so they had to be very strong swimmers and a love of water was uppermost in the breed's foundation. This ancestral instinct was obviously still in Katy. Retrieving and water were strong in her mind and I wasn't going to be the one to tell her that she'd got it all wrong. Water wasn't the only thing Katy was interested in. Liquid of any type attracted her little black nose. Katy had only been with us a day or two when we discovered her love of alcohol.

The dogs are normally restricted to the dog room, which is off the kitchen, and the kitchen itself, but in the evenings when Don and I have finished our work, they're allowed to come into the lounge. They all settle down very well. You would probably think, with five dogs about the place, we could hardly move. But not at all. They have their own little niche and stick to it. Their "own little niche" being mainly the furniture, I must admit, but there is just enough room for all of us, as long as we don't get any visitors who want to sit down!

Teak, Bracken and Mocha line up on the settee. Buttons usually sleeps curled up by the radiator. It's always difficult to relax and watch television when there's a puppy about the place, but Katy had curled up on the floor by the settee so I felt I could give my full attention to the thriller film on television. Don was sitting in his usual chair on the other side of the fireplace and, as he often does when sitting down and relaxing, he'd fetched a bottle of beer from the pantry, poured half into his pewter mug and left it on the hearth. I was sitting on the edge of my seat, engrossed in the television set. Yet another woman had been murdered. We had three suspects to choose from — the solicitor, the psychiatrist and the policeman. In the back of my mind, a little alarm bell rang. I tried to drag my attention away from the film. I could hear a lapping noise. I looked round quickly. All the dogs appeared to be in place on the settee and I could see Katy's tail under the coffee table. She was obviously fast asleep there. I turned my attention back to the television.

"Who do you think's done it?" Don asked, as the adverts came on and he reached down for his pot of beer, took a drink and then looked into the pot with a worried expression on his face.

"I don't know. I think it's the policeman," I said.

Don poured the rest of the bottle of beer into his pint pot and placed it on the hearth beside his chair. The next time the alarm bell rang in the back of my mind, I ignored it. The film was just coming to its conclusion.

"Well, I would never have believed it was the psychiatrist." I turned and looked at Don as the film titles rolled up the screen. Again, he was staring into his pint pot in amazement. He put it down on the coffee table in front of him and scratched the back of his head. "What's the matter?" I asked. "Is the beer off?"

"No . . . I can't understand it. I'm sure I haven't drunk a whole bottle of beer, but every time I pick my pot up it seems to be empty. Am I going mad? Well, I must have drunk it," he said, as he went to the pantry for another bottle. "I don't feel as if I have, though," he muttered on the way.

Katy was stretched out on the settee next to Teak, eyes tightly shut, her back legs twitching a little. Then, suddenly, *thump!* she'd rolled off the settee and on to the floor and lay there with her paws up in the air, mouth half open. I rushed across to her, thinking that she looked almost dead.

"Katy! Katy! Are you all right?"

She rolled over slowly and sat up, opening bleary eyes, and hiccuped. Don stood stock still, his bottle of beer in one hand, opener in the other, staring at her. She hiccuped again.

"That dog's drunk," he said.

"Don't be silly. She can't be drunk."

He knelt down on the floor and sniffed at Katy's breath. "That dog is stoned out of her tiny little mind," he announced with a smile on his face. "Thank heavens for that! I thought I was going mad. She's been drinking my beer all night."

I even had to move the bottles from the drinks' trolley, when I discovered Katy trying to prise the top off a bottle of sherry.

As Katy's character unfurled, so did my love for her. I had been afraid, at first, that I wouldn't be able to love her, not for a long time. The memory of Shadow was still in the forefront of my mind and I couldn't stop myself wishing that the black Labrador in the house was still Shadow. Katy, being the dog she was, must have sensed my grief, for she did her utmost to win me over. Each evening, she climbed onto my knee and proclaimed her undying love for me by trying to lick my chin, my nose and my ears. Then, with a satisfied sigh, she'd curl up there and refuse to move.

Within a matter of days, I was returning her affection. Her little antics were so completely different from any other dog I'd owned that I began to realize Katy and I had a very special relationship blossoming. I could never be annoyed with her, not for long, because whenever she did something naughty, she was always so sorry about it afterwards. She would come and appeal with her dark brown eyes and enormous ears that would flick to and fro, listening for my forgiving tone. I realized immediately that I must never shout at Katy.

Most of the time, Katy would not leave my side, but sit waiting to have a game with me or just to be picked up and loved. So, on the odd occasion when I looked down and she had disappeared, I knew she was engrossed in some new mischief. I was making mince pies to put in the freezer for Christmas and Katy had been sitting quietly at my feet, catching any crumbs of pastry that came her way. I was so engrossed in my baking that I had forgotten to look down for at least fifteen minutes. I suddenly realized she was no longer there. I shook the surplus flour from my hands and went to investigate. The lounge was covered normally with a red patterned carpet but as I peeped in, it was a totally different shade that met my eyes. It had been transformed from a dull red to brilliant yellows, pinks and oranges. There had been two vases full of chrysanthemums on the hearth. Katy had taken every flower out of its vase and pulled each petal off, and was now having the time of her life rolling in the petals and throwing them up in the air. Seeing the empty stalks there and Katy delirious with joy, I wanted to laugh, but that would have been a terrible mistake. I bit my lip and managed to say, "Oh, Katy!" in a sad and disapproving tone. She sat bolt upright and stared at me for a moment and then slunk, with her belly close to the ground, and hid under Don's armchair.

I felt really mean. I wanted to join in her fun and throw the petals about myself. It seemed cruel to stop her having such a wonderful time but I realized if I gave in now, Katy would be left with the impression that she had been given carte blanche to chew anything and everything, and next time the article may not be so easily replaceable as a vase of chrysanthemums. She watched me clear away the petals from her hiding place, such a miserable expression on her face that I felt sorry for her. As soon as the carpet was returned to its dull red, I felt forgiveness was in order and retrieved the knotted tights I always carried around in my pocket.

"What's this, Katy? Let's have a game!"

She was out instantly, overjoyed that I had released her from her penance.

Katy reminded me so much of Emma. Although Emma was eighteen months old when we met, she still had all her puppyish ways. She loved carrying things in her mouth and would nuzzle me with her cold nose to ask me to put my hand out to receive her present. I'd hear her bounce up and down with excitement, waiting for me to throw her toy. She was very extravagant with her squeaky toys, which she absolutely adored, and would spend a day, maybe two, retrieving them. And, then, she'd suddenly decide that she was fed up with that particular toy and she'd chew it into tiny little pieces and would give me no peace until we called at the pet shop for another one.

In the day, I hardly had time to grieve for Emma, especially now Katy needed all my attention, but the nights were lonely and silent. There was no dog to share our bedroom and those old familiar dreams, or nightmares, recurred. It was always the same dream. I was in Nottingham, alone, surrounded by crowds of people and heavy traffic. I couldn't see and I didn't have Emma. I used to wake up in a cold sweat, sit up and listen and when I heard Emma snoring peacefully in her bed, I could go back to sleep. But now there was silence from the bottom of the radiator, where Emma's bed had always been.

"It's no good," I said to Don one morning. "We must take a dog to bed. I just can't sleep without those rhythmic snores of a Labrador."

Don could sleep through anything, but at least he understood my feelings.

"Well, why not take Bracken? I'm sure he'd think it was a real treat."

That night, Bracken took up his usual place on the settee, head on the cushion, eyes closed.

"Bracken, come on, up to bed!"

He opened one bleary eye and ignored me.

"You can come upstairs and sleep with us."

He opened the other eye, lifted his head slightly, sniffed the air and put his head back down on the cushion again. It took me about ten minutes of persuasion and cajoling to get Bracken off the settee and upstairs into our bedroom. I had placed a bed for him at the bottom of the radiator. He looked at it suspiciously.

"Bracken!" I ordered him. "On your bed!"

He backed off and eyed me with disgust. Don climbed into bed and put his arms around me.

"Leave him alone, he'll settle."

Don kissed me goodnight and within minutes was breathing heavily, fast asleep. I lay awake, listening to Bracken pacing the floor. Every night was the same. Bracken showed more and more reluctance to come and join us in the bedroom. I couldn't understand it. I was offering him a luxury.

The crunch came one night when he actually growled at me. I'd never heard Bracken growl in his life. I stepped back in total astonishment. My instinct was to grab him by the scruff of the neck and tell him that he never, ever growled at me. But then, suddenly, I realized what was happening in his mind. He had always worshipped Emma and when she died he missed her, and now I was asking him to sleep in her place. He couldn't accept that. To him, Emma had been the leader of the pack and I can only imagine he saw it as a sort of sacrilege to sleep in her place.

CHAPTER THREE

FETCH, KATY!

"Don't do that, Katy!" Kerensa said, pushing Katy away from her favourite toy rabbit, Hazel. Katy took no notice and proceeded to try and drag one of Hazel's ears off. "Stop it!" Kerensa persisted.

I prised Katy's teeth gently off the stuffed rabbit's ear and told her that was definitely taboo. My heart went out to Kerensa. She'd had many a cuddly toy stolen and shredded by the dogs. The panda was the worst. I hadn't seen Katy sneak upstairs and retrieve the large, cuddly panda from the end of Kerensa's bed. I can't lay all the blame on Katy. Although she was the instigator, Teak did the real damage. The pair of them sneaked out of the back door, onto the back lawn, and tore the panda to bits.

I don't know whether you've ever seen inside the cuddly toys we buy nowadays, but they are stuffed with tiny little pieces of foam . . . millions and millions of tiny little pieces of foam. If it had been a nice calm day, it would have made my job a lot easier. But it wasn't. It was November and there was a blustery gale. I was just making our mid-morning cup of tea in the kitchen and I happened to glance out of the window. I thought it was snowing, except the flakes seemed rather large. I went out into the garden to discover that it wasn't raining cats and dogs, but pieces of panda! It was a physical impossibility to collect all the bits. Every time I managed to get a few on my shovel, the wind came and hurled them away. I often wonder how far Kerensa's panda travelled that day.

"Are you going to train Katy today? What are we going to do?" Kerensa asked.

"I think I'll teach her to wait, and then she'll be able to go out in the car."

"Can I help?"

"No, not really, Kerensa. Perhaps you could fetch Bicky." (That was Kerensa's toy dog on wheels.) "And you can train him to wait."

She rushed upstairs and brought Bicky down into the kitchen. She insisted that Bicky wore the exact type of collar and lead I had put on Katy. A very soft leather collar and lightweight lead should be used on a small puppy. I had never had any problems with any of the Labradors on collar and lead training. They just took to it automatically. Kerensa stood with Bicky on her left-hand side.

"Now what do I do?" she asked.

"Just a minute while I put Katy's collar on." I sat Katy on my left. "Tell him to wait," I instructed Kerensa, and gave Katy the same command. I took one small step to the right and stepped back immediately. "There's a clever girl," I told Katy. It was so quick, she hadn't had chance to move from her sit position. The first lesson had been won.

Kerensa was still standing next to Bicky. "Well, what did you do?" she asked me.

"I only took one pace away," I said, "and then straight back."

"That's not waiting." Kerensa had been used to seeing the other dogs wait for minutes on end while I walked a long way from them.

"But Katy and Bicky are only babies," I explained to her.

"You can't expect them to wait for a long time, not until they really understand what it means."

As Kerensa took a pace to her right, she forgot to lengthen her lead out and Bicky fell over with the pressure. "You stupid dog!" she scolded.

"No, he's not stupid at all. That was your fault. You pulled him over with the lead, Kerensa. You must keep a slack lead if you want him to do as you tell him." I could see Kerensa was going to lose her patience, so I showed her again with Katy. I sat her on my left and made sure the lead was hanging down loosely. "Wait!" I took one pace to the right, counted two seconds and stepped back and knelt down on the floor to give her praise. Kerensa followed suit, this time succeeding with her dog on wheels. I am sure we have the best trained stuffed dog on wheels, for whenever I trained the dogs, Kerensa trained Bicky. He's marvellous at staying. He's not too brilliant on retrieving though.

"Mummy, can I go in the dog room to Katy?"

"No, definitely not," I told Kerensa. The dog room was absolutely forbidden to children.

"Oh, please. I only want to go and stroke her."

"No, Kerensa. You know the rules. You can stroke her in a minute when I let her out."

I have always stuck firmly to the belief that the dogs should have a place of sanctuary, not only away from Kerensa or other calling children, but from us too. A place where they can feel safe to sleep in peace. I know Kerensa would never deliberately harm one of the dogs, but children tend to look upon pets as their toys. When Kerensa was younger, I would often find her poking her fingers down ears and up noses and in eyes, which is just a child's curiosity. Although I had always told Kerensa that it was wrong to poke and pull, I realized that I couldn't expect a little toddler to understand and to curb her natural curiosity. So, from the very beginning, I decided that the dogs would have a place where Kerensa was not allowed.

It works extremely well. It means that when I have time to watch everyone, Kerensa can play with the dogs, especially in the garden. She loves throwing a ball for them. But when the dogs need to sleep, or I have other things to attend to, then they're put in the dog room out of harm's way. I have so often seen young children tormenting their pets to death and parents not taking any action to prevent them. If you are able to put yourself in the dog's position, think how intolerable it would be to be closed away in a room where you are unable to escape and to be tormented by a child who's pulling your tail, your ears, hitting you and pushing you about. Wouldn't you retaliate in the end? I know I would. Although I've never known any of my Labradors show any aggression whatsoever, there's always the chance that it could happen, so I never give either Kerensa or dogs the opportunity to be left together unsupervised.

Kerensa had moved the kitchen stool towards the dog room door so that she could climb up and watch the dogs, who were, by this time, getting excited. It was Sunday morning and we were going on our big walk into the park and round the woods. It was Katy's first day out with all the other dogs. As Don took the leads down from the hook in the hall, he asked me, "Are you sure Katy will be all right? She won't leap out of the car will she?"

"I'm positive," I said.

I had spent the whole week training Katy not to jump out of the back of the car when it was opened. It's extremely important that, having five dogs, complete discipline must reign all the time. I can imagine the chaos that would be caused if our dogs dashed out of the car at the first opportunity. Katy was actually far too small to make the jump from the back to the ground but, nevertheless, I'd trained her that she must sit and wait until I told her she could get out of the car.

Kerensa jumped into the back seat of the car. "Oh, Katy's in the back. She's nibbling Teak's ears," she told Don, as he backed the car down the drive. "Now she's biting Mocha."

"She won't hurt them, Kerensa. Don't worry."

All the way to the park we were treated to a running commentary of what Katy was doing. I must admit, I was a little worried as Don unlocked the car door and enforced the command to wait. Katy was so excited. Would she remember her training? She sat there, her dark brown eyes full of anticipation, patiently waiting, until I lifted her out and placed her on the ground. Each dog was called from the car by name and then told to sit, until given the command, "Off you go."

Katy was so impatient. I couldn't expect a young puppy of twelve weeks to sit as still as the other dogs, so I held her collar, re-enforcing, "Sit, Katy, and wait. There's a good girl."

The grass and trees were calling to her little puppy mind, with the promise of soft earth under her paws. A thousand scents, as variegated to a dog as the shades of green are to the human eye. Katy did her best to keep her bottom firmly on the ground, but her two front paws were dancing. I could understand just how she felt, for I still have the delight of discovering things, even though my sight was restored several years ago. I still feel the thrill of discovery as I look at the birds and the trees and the grass. I wanted to run and jump and shout, to pick the dead leaves up and throw them in the air — but I had to be content with watching Katy do it. As she ran away from me, my heart ran with her. She skipped and barked and rolled with the joy of new life.

Controlling five dogs is no easy task. On those days when Don can't take the dogs out, I prefer to spread the load and do two walks. Teak, Bracken and now Katy on the first walk. Buttons and Mocha on the second. It's impossible for me to watch five dogs at once, only having one seeing eye. The incredible thing is the dogs know I can't see very far, especially Buttons, who takes full advantage of this fact.

"Where's Buttons gone?" I asked Don, looking round for her.

"Oh, I don't know!" he said with a sigh. "She was here a minute ago."

We both stood and looked round, knowing that only food would tempt Buttons away from us. We both called her. All the other dogs came back immediately, sitting and looking up at us questioningly.

"Where's Buttons?" I asked Bracken. But he ignored me. "I bet she's gone onto that tip."

Don looked towards the woods where, concealed among the trees, was a tip. Food was often to be found there.

"I'll go and have a look," Kerensa shouted, running up the bank and peering through the trees. "Yes, there she is, Daddy. I can see her. She's eating something."

Don and I both knew it was pointless calling her. When food was on offer, Buttons was deaf to everything else. The best way of dealing with her was to sneak up at the back, grab her by the scruff of the neck and give her a good shake.

"You horrible dog, Buttons," I told her, as I caught up with her. "One of these days, you'll be poisoned."

Buttons gave me one of her sulky, defiant looks and followed me slowly back down the slope, onto the park. I don't profess to be an expert on all dogs, but I know my dogs inside out and Buttons is craftier than a cartload of monkeys. If I watch her constantly, I can keep her with me and I can tell by the expression on her face and the way she lowers her body to the ground that somewhere there's food. "Buttons, *no!*" I call and she'll immediately turn and trot back. It has now reached the stage where I watch Buttons, and Buttons watches me. I only have to take my eyes off her for one second and she's gone.

The Labradors don't normally range out but tend to hang around. Teak, on the other hand, is gone in a flash. But then she's back in a flash too, so there's no worry. The German shorthaired pointers' instinct is to range into the distance, to circle and then return.

Kerensa was having the time of her life. She was playing "tiggy" with the dogs. "You're on, Bracken," she said, as she touched his ear and ran away. "Caught you, Mocha," she giggled, patting Mocha on the neck. Mocha, who wasn't quite sure what all the fuss was about, threw herself into the air with gay abandon, landed on the grass and went straight off into one of her daydreams. I'm sure that I shall never, ever meet a dog like Mocha. I don't have any fear of upsetting her feelings when I tell you that she's totally brainless. If Mocha could speak, her reaction to that comment would be, Oh, do you really think so? How nice of you! Most of her days — and nights for that matter — are spent dreaming. Sitting, gazing into the distance with a look of total vacancy in her chestnut brown eyes. Often, when I call her by name and she's listening, she'll just jump up and down on the spot, with all her four feet off the ground at the same moment. I'm here . . . I'm here! she grins at you, throwing herself up and down.

"Right, is everybody ready?" Don called. He had pulled the rubber ring from his pocket. Oh, joy of joys! The dogs galloped round, barking madly. It was retrieve games. I wondered what Katy would think of this. We always take a large rubber ring with us to throw for the dogs. It can be retrieved easily and they can all get round and play tug-of-war.

Teak can leap from a standstill to six foot in the air and as soon as Don produces the rubber ring, Teak leaps at him, nudging him on the ear or pushing her nose at the back of his neck and making a swipe for his cap. The Labradors stick strictly to ground level, waiting for the ring to be thrown.

"Off you go!" Don shouted, as he threw the ring into the air.

Teak always reaches the ring before anyone else, but she's not in the slightest bit interested in retrieving it. Her motto is "leave the retrieving to the retrievers", but she does enjoy the feeling of speed, the excitement of the chase. She circles the article in wild gallops until one of the Labradors picks it up, then rushes back to Don and waits for the next throw. Buttons wouldn't even bother chasing it. She sits and watches the others. So does Mocha, who really can't understand why the dogs rush off and rush back.

Katy came back with the rubber ring, much to my surprise. "How did you get that, you little dog?" I asked her, as she brought it to my feet.

Don was laughing. "She'll teach them a thing or two as she grows older. You watch how she retrieves it." He picked it up and threw it again.

Teak and Bracken raced off, with Katy following. Katy had realized that Teak, being the fastest, would get there first, so her aim was to stop Teak. She made grabs for her. Anywhere would do . . . an ear, a back leg, a neck. Instead of turning round and giving Katy what for, Teak tried to shake her off . . . unsuccessfully. Consequently, Teak and Katy arrived at the rubber ring at the same moment. Katy was beneath Teak's paws. She grabbed the rubber ring from under Bracken's nose and was racing back to us before the other two had time to realize what had happened. Bracken looked around on the grass with astonishment and then up in the air.

"Bracken," I shouted, waving the ring at him. "It's here!"
He came galloping back, determined the next retrieve

would be his. He got so annoyed with Katy that he barked and ran round her in circles when, yet again, the rubber ring was hers.

Getting to know Katy was as exciting as looking through a kaleidoscope, for one moment she was chasing the ring and the next she had dropped it and was racing across the park.

"Katy!" I called. "Where's she going?" I asked Don.

"Don't know," he said, getting out his dog whistle and giving it a good blow. No response.

"Is there another dog over there?" I asked him. She'd now gone out of my sight.

"No, there's a football match going on. Where the devil is she going?"

I ran off in the direction I'd last seen Katy. "Katy! Katy, come back. What have I got?" I tried all my tricks of leaping up and down and clapping my hands and then putting them into my pocket to extract the chocolate drops, but no Katy. As I neared the football match I saw her, sitting at a boy's feet, pressing her body on his legs and looking up at him with adoration.

"Katy, what are you doing?"

She ignored me completely, as if she'd never even seen me before and this young boy she'd found was her long lost owner. I was tempted to let her see how annoyed I was and tell her off, but then I thought about it more carefully. No, she liked people. That was always a good characteristic in a dog. Perhaps, if I showed anger, she would be afraid to go to people. But I still wanted her to understand that this wasn't the done thing. I picked her up gently.

"You bad puppy," I told her. "You nearly gave me a heart attack running off like that." I tried to keep my voice calm and low. Her ears flew back and I could feel her body stiffening. "It's all right," I said, "but you could have been run over if there'd been a road there, couldn't you now?"

44

Her tail began to wag furiously and her little pink tongue licked round my hands. Life with Katy certainly wouldn't be dull and I couldn't wait for her to show me yet another side of her character.

CHAPTER FOUR

THE DOG TRAINING CLUB

Katy was four months old. Just the right time to enrol her in a dog training club. Our local one had closed as the room was needed for other functions but Tracey, who worked for me, helping me with paperwork, housework, dogs — in fact, a general dogsbody — had found another club not too far away.

"They meet on Tuesday evening," she said, "at half past seven, I think." She, too, had acquired a new puppy, a working sheepdog called Cedar. "I'd like to take Cedar anyway, so I'll come and pick you up at about seven o'clock."

Katy would need to be well and truly socialized with other dogs if I was to take her to the obedience shows, where she'd be expected to work in close proximity to many different breeds. For anyone like myself, who loves dogs and their training, a night at the dog training club is an exciting occasion. I couldn't wait to meet all the new people and their dogs and, hopefully, glean advice and new training methods from the instructor.

As I pushed the door into the hall open, my ears were bombarded by barking. The hall, not very large, just managed to contain the fifteen handlers and dogs that were sitting around the perimeter.

"Good grief!" Tracey yelled. "What a din! Obviously the trainer isn't here yet or she'd do something about it."

All the other dog clubs I'd ever attended were reasonably peaceful, the trainers taking immediate action with any noisy dogs.

"Let's go and sit down there." Tracey pointed to two free seats at the far end of the hall. "Perhaps it won't be quite so noisy."

From the look of things, most of the owners appeared to be raw beginners. The man three seats down from us was getting rather annoyed with his dog. He yelled and yanked at it.

"Edward, leave it alone." His German shepherd-cross dog was trying to demolish a Yorkshire terrier.

Tracey looked at her watch. "Nearly half past. Let's hope she hurries up and comes."

Even Katy didn't like the noise. She sat under my chair, her ears flattened to her head, the loose skin above her eyes furrowed, making her look more like a bloodhound than a Labrador puppy. I can't say I hadn't noticed the woman up the other end of the hall. I could hardly miss her. But I certainly hadn't put her down as the trainer, for she was having more trouble with her boxer than all the others put together. So, when she handed the dog over to someone sitting next to her and marched into the centre of the hall, my heart sank.

She clapped her hands together in an effort to make herself heard. "Good evening. Now, for those of you who are new 'ere tonight, I would like to tell you straight away that my name is Ethel. I don't run a formal club 'ere. We should all be on first name terms."

She stood about five foot tall and, at a rough guess, would have topped the scales at fifteen stone. She wore orange slacks and a sweater to match, which made her look like a Jaffa orange on legs. Her head was swathed in a thick, brown, woolly scarf, pulled tightly over her ears and round her neck, the tassels dancing on her ample bosom.

"Ethel!" her boxer-holding friend called nervously. "He's eating the floorboards."

Ethel, who had a very strong Derbyshire accent, didn't hold with using aitches. "Let 'im 'ave that packet of chocolate bourbons in me bag. That'll keep 'im 'appy." She turned her back on the boxer. "Yes, where was I? Ah, 'ands up those with problems. Don't worry, we shall 'ave all of them solved before the night's out. You, over there." She pointed a sausage-shaped finger to a young blonde girl with a black and white mongrel dog. The girl stepped out onto the floor, with the dog bouncing up and down at her side like a rubber ball, making grabs for her hand. "Now then, mi' duck, wot's your problem?" Ethel folded her arms in underneath her bosom.

"He will keep jumping up and down and he bites my hand. I've tried everything. Nothing seems to work," the girl said.

"Mmm, yes . . . that's easy to solve," Ethel announced with confidence. "When 'e jumps up, 'it 'im on the 'ead. An' wear thick gloves."

"Will that stop him biting me?" the girl asked.

"No . . ." Ethel smiled. "But it won't 'urt you then, will it?"

I turned to look at Tracey, who was sitting biting her bottom lip — a sure sign that any moment she was going to burst into hysterics. "Am I hearing right?" I said to her. "Did she really tell that girl to ''it it on the 'ead'?" I mimicked. Tracey nodded. "Poor thing." My hand went underneath the chair to stroke Katy's ears. I somehow felt she'd heard and understood the advice given and would need reassurance that she wouldn't get hit on the head.

Edward's owner was the next victim. He was launched onto the floor by his dog. "Bones is my trouble," he boomed.

"Whenever I give him a bone, he won't let me within three yards of him. Snarls! Real vicious he is."

Ethel closed her eyes and rested her treble chin in one of her stumpy hands, as if thinking deeply. "Don't give 'im any bones," she advised.

Tracey had buried her head in her anorak but I could still hear the giggles.

A very sweet looking miniature poodle walked daintily onto the floor, followed by her middle-aged owner. "I've been coming for some time now," the poodle's owner said, "but I still can't get him to retrieve a dumbbell."

"Well, 'aven't you been doing wot I told you last week, Brenda?"

"No, I haven't actually," Brenda replied quietly. "I didn't like the thought of doing that. It seems cruel to me."

"Cruel . . . *cruel!*" Ethel screeched, with a pitch that would have put a fighting tom-cat to shame. "Give 'im 'ere. I'll show yer 'ow to do it." She snatched the lead of the poodle out of Brenda's hand and produced a roll of bandage from her pocket. "Give us yer dumbbell."

Brenda hesitated before handing the dumbbell over. Tracey and I sat in stunned silence. No doubt Tracey was wondering the same as I: what was Ethel going to do with a poodle, a dumbbell and a roll of bandage? Ethel sat on the floor, grabbed the poodle by the scruff of the neck and, stuffing it between her fat knees, she pushed the dumbbell in its mouth. She then wrapped the bandage around the dog's nose, making sure it was securely tied so that the dog couldn't open its mouth.

"Easy, in't it?" She looked at Brenda, who stood helplessly watching. "You only 'ave to do this ten minutes every day an' your dog'll never drop the dumbbell again."

"I don't believe it," I muttered. "How could anybody be so stupid? Why doesn't Brenda stop her from doing it? I wouldn't let her do that to my dog."

49

"Some people don't know any better," Tracey replied. "If this is the only dog club Brenda's ever been to, she must think Ethel's right."

I tried to make myself inconspicuous, holding my handbag in front of me, hoping not to attract Ethel's attention. I didn't want any of her advice.

"You," she said. "Wot's your problem?"

Tracey gave me a nudge with her elbow. "Go on, I dare you. Stand up and tell her your problems."

I stood up. "I don't have any," I announced.

"I can see one from 'ere," she said, pointing down at Katy and then looking round the room to make sure that everyone was watching. "Wot about 'er collar?"

Katy was wearing a soft leather collar, and she sat angelically under my chair. "What about it?"

"That is a leather collar, if my eyes don't deceive me."

"So it is," I agreed.

"You shouldn't 'ave that dog on a leather collar. It should be on a check-chain like all the others. No dog is allowed in my training club unless it's wearing a check-chain collar. Perhaps you'll remember that for next week."

I was horrified at the thought of putting my poor little Katy on a check-chain collar. Ethel might have been bigger than me — at least sideways — but I wasn't going to let her browbeat me. "I couldn't possibly put this puppy on a check-chain. She's only four months old. It would make her hard and probably ruin her for the rest of her life."

"Rubbish!" Ethel stamped her foot on the wooden floorboards. "You've obviously never owned a dog before in your life." She proceeded to lecture me on the merits of check-chain collars while her boxer, having finished the cream bourbons, was ripping the floorboards up again.

"I'm not stopping here to be insulted," I told Tracey as I sat down. "Come on, let's go."

"Not likely!" Tracey giggled. "I haven't had such an exciting night out for years."

"That's it!" Ethel announced with a smug smile on her face. "I've sorted all your problems out. Now we'll 'ave some 'eel work. The first four up, please."

Four dogs hurled themselves with eager enthusiasm onto the floor. Ethel had backed off to her original position at the top of the room and began to shout out commands.

"FORWARD! ABOUT TURN! HALT!"

The four dogs were having a whale of a time, dragging their owners this way and that.

"Why doesn't she stop them?" I asked Tracey. "And show them how to train their dogs properly? After all, that's what they've paid for."

"Why doesn't she stop them?" Tracey repeated. "Because she doesn't know how. That woman couldn't train ivy up a wall."

The pandemonium stopped temporarily when Ethel announced it was tea-break time. Coffee, tea and crisps would be on sale.

"'Ere, Madge —" She turned to her friend. "— take Bruno for a walk while I deal with this lot. Mind 'im in next door's garden, he nearly 'ad their cat last week."

I felt quite sorry for Madge. She was a small, very slightly built lady with greying hair, a tiny little pointed nose and very delicate hands. Not the type of person one imagined on the other end of the lead from a bouncing boxer. I think Bruno had recognized the word "cat". He was so excited at the prospect of getting into next door's garden that he took one huge leap to the hall door. Poor little Madge lost her footing on the slippery boards and sailed headlong after him. Fifteen minutes later, Madge had still not returned. Ethel was quite unperturbed. Sitting at the top of the hall, she was approaching her third packet of crisps.

"Do you think something's happened?" I asked Tracey. "It surely doesn't take fifteen minutes for a boxer to spend a penny."

"It depends where he wanted to spend it." Tracey grinned at me. "Come on, let's go and see if we can find out what's happening."

She led the way across the hall. Ethel spotted us.

"Training's starting now. Where are you going?"

I felt as if I'd been accused of a murder, by the tone of her voice.

"Erm . . . err . . ." I stammered. "I'm just going to take my puppy out."

"Well, don't be long," she boomed, "or you'll miss everything."

The thought of missing everything didn't exactly grieve me. It was quite dark outside, so I had to rely on Tracey's interpretation of what was happening in next door's garden. Little Madge was crouched down next to the privet hedge, moaning quietly to herself, a collar and lead clasped in her hand . . . but no Bruno. I didn't need to see to know what was happening. There were howls and yelps, along with blood-curdling cat screams.

Tracey put her hand on Madge's shoulder. "What's happened?"

The poor little woman jumped visibly. "Oh, he'll kill it. He won't come back until it's dead."

"Has he done this sort of thing before?" I questioned Madge.

"Yes, there isn't a live cat left on our street."

"Why didn't you make her bring him out, if you know he's so bad?"

The poor little woman began to cry. "I'm all on my own since our Fred passed away last Christmas. I live next door to Ethel, you see, and she's sort of taken over. She said it would do me good to come out to the dog club."

"I've a good mind to go back in there and give her what for," I said, trying to sound braver than I felt.

Madge grasped at my arm. "Oh, don't do that, love. I have to live next door to her. She'll never forgive me for this. Help me get him back."

As luck would have it, the cat had managed to escape up an apple tree, leaving Bruno scratching at the bark and howling mournfully. Tracey grasped Bruno's collar and lead and pushed her way through the privet hedge. Luckily for Tracey, Bruno didn't have the same attitude to humans as he did to cats. As soon as Tracey approached him, he dived on her and then tried to lick her to death. We let Madge lead Bruno back into the hall, sworn to secrecy.

Ethel was just announcing the final exercise. "We'll have you all up on the floor, in a circle."

"Go on, get in there." Tracey tried to push me into the circle.

"Not likely. Katy would have a heart attack and it wouldn't do my nerves a lot of good. Anyway, what about you?" But Ethel had spotted us.

"You two . . . come on! You're the only ones sitting out. You 'aven't done nowt this evening. Let's 'ave you!"

Tracey was giggling again. I had to think quickly. "Oh, we can't join in tonight . . . Katy's hurt her foot. We only came to watch."

She snorted in my direction, turned her back on me and began to yell the commands above the din of barking. Three of the dogs decided they'd had enough training for one evening and, instead of walking by their handlers' heels, they launched into a three-way fight. For a moment, I thought Ethel was going to take action at last. When she threw her arms up into the air, I expected her to rush down the room and sort the dogs out. Instead, she clamped her hands over her ears and then turned and trotted out of the hall as fast as her weight would allow. I was sorely tempted to do the same.

"This isn't a dog training club, it's a canine nightmare."

The three dog owners, having completely lost control over their pets, stood in silent horror.

"Oh, come on, Tracey. I can't stand this any longer. You get that black and white thing and I'll try and get the other two." We left our respective puppies sitting under the chairs. "If you get hold of them behind their ears, on the scruff of the neck," I instructed Tracey, "they won't bite you."

It's quite pointless shouting or hitting a fighting dog. He will only think his opponent is attacking him from behind and will dive in with more fury than ever. I knew, only too well, that if my hands got in the way they'd be torn to shreds. Tracey and I, miraculously unscathed, returned the dogs to their owners and advised them to keep them as far apart as possible for the rest of the evening.

"That is definitely it," I told Tracey. "I'm going."

"Yes, I've had enough," she agreed, and we collected our dogs from under our seats.

As we left the hall, we saw Ethel outside, hands still clamped to her ears. I was tempted to inform her that we had sorted out the fighting and she could safely return, but I decided against it, thinking that dogs and handlers were far better off without Ethel there.

"Well, that was a waste of a Tuesday evening," Tracey commented as she got into the car.

"Not exactly. If we hadn't have been there, what would have happened to those dogs? But I certainly won't be coming again next Tuesday."

It's a disturbing thought that there may be other dog clubs like that, and other Ethels. And how are the dog-owning public to know that these methods are totally alien? The only bit of advice I can give is that training dogs should be based on practice, patience and praise.

CHAPTER FIVE

IN THE HOT SEAT

I am one of those unfortunate people who spends more than they earn. However much or little my yearly income is, I well exceed it, so a call from my bank is dreaded. I have promised myself that when I get a statement that's completely in the black, I shall invite the bank manager to dinner.

"Mrs Hocken?" a strange voice asked on the telephone.

"Yes."

"This is the bank. I feel that it's time you came in to discuss your account."

I didn't recognize the man's voice. It wasn't the usual bank manager. "That's not Mr Nestling, is it?"

"No . . . no. Mr Nestling left last week. I'm taking over temporarily until the new manager comes. But I do feel, Mrs Hocken, that we should get your account sorted out for him."

"Yes," I admitted, with a sinking feeling. "I do have a bit of an overdraft, don't I?"

"Overdraft! I would have referred to it as a tornado," he chuckled.

I didn't think that it was at all funny. I arranged to take my place in the hot seat at two-thirty that afternoon. I tried desperately to think of something I could tell him that would appease him. Was I having any books coming out? Did

anybody owe me any money? Being a writer, I never knew
from one year to the next what my income would be. I
couldn't think of anything that would reassure him, except
hope, which is what I live on most of the time. I knew, from
past experience, the best policy was to sound convincing.

"Would you like a lift down to the bank?" Don asked me,
when lunch was over. "I haven't got an appointment until
five o'clock."

"No thank you, I'd much rather walk. I think I'll take
Bracken with me for moral support. I feel half-naked if I go
out without a dog and, anyway, this temporary bank
manager might like dogs and seeing Bracken could take his
mind off my money troubles."

I sat in the bank, gazing fixedly at the manager's door,
waiting for the summons. I always expect bank managers to
look well-fed, clean, tidy and assured, so I was a little
disappointed when I saw my adversary for the first time as
he heaved open the big oak door into his office.

"Mrs Hocken?" he questioned in a tremulous voice. "My
name is Barrowby." He was about to proffer his hand for a
shake but then saw Bracken and withdrew it immediately.
He stood tall, thin and lanky, his sports jacket cuffs finishing
a long way before his wrists, his thick, horn-rimmed glasses
resting halfway down a long, bony nose. As in the case of so
many self-conscious people, his glasses were a constant
source of irritation to him. He'd altered their position on his
nose three times before we were seated in his office. I
immediately felt one up. He was more nervous than I was.

"Now then, Mr Barrowby —" I launched into my defence.
"I don't think you have any need to worry about my
overdraft. I've always paid up in the past, haven't I?"

"That isn't the point, Mrs Hocken. Do you know how
much bank interest rates are these days?" His large, goldfish
eyes darted between me and Bracken. I had made a mistake
this time. The presence of a dog, rather than pouring oil on

troubled waters, stirred this poor man up into a frenzy of terror. I shook my head. "I have here . . ." He picked up a thick folder ". . . your last year's accounts. What are we going to do about them?"

What did he expect me to do about them? I couldn't change them now.

"Look at these electricity bills, for instance. They're astronomical."

"You can hardly blame me for the over-priced electricity," I told him.

He flashed a look of disgust at me over his glasses. "I just don't know what to do about it," he said, leafing through my folder. "Do you know how much money you spent in dog food and vets' bills last year?"

"No."

"Then I'll tell you." Mr Barrowby pointed his pen at me.

"I'd rather you didn't. It would only upset me."

He put his hands to the side of his forehead and gradually his head fell further and further down, until it hit the desk.

Good grief, I thought. He's had a heart attack. What do I do? I was just about to summon help, when his head shot up into the air again.

"Mrs Hocken, you can't always act like an ostrich." He thumped the desk with his fist and the pens in their holder did a dance.

I looked at the clock. I couldn't think of anything better to do. Five minutes. Was that all? I felt as if I'd been in there for a week.

My song of courage began to echo in my mind: "Where was Moses when the light went out? Down the cellar with his shirt hanging out." I may show a brave face, but inside I was absolutely terrified. But I'd been brought up never to show fear or helplessness. My mum had taught me the lines about Moses when I was eight.

We lived in an old shop, with cellars that housed the

electricity and gas meters and coal. We all had to take our turn at putting the shilling in the meter, or fetching some more coal for the fire. I was terror-stricken when it came to my turn to go down to the cellar. It was dark and damp and horrible. I couldn't see anything down there, so I imagined ghosts, ghouls and skeletons. They were all waiting for me down in the cellar.

When it was my turn, my mum would stand at the top of the cellar steps. Trying to encourage me to conquer my fear, she would say, "Run down and we'll both sing 'Where was Moses when the light went out? Down the cellar with his shirt hanging out.'"

I already felt braver.

"Don't worry about it, Mr Barrowby. I don't!"

His head hit the desk again and for a long time it stayed there, giving me ample opportunity to examine the bald spot on the top of his head. "Mrs Hocken," he mumbled from the file. "I haven't slept for three nights trying to sort out your account."

"Why don't you leave it until the new bank manager comes?" I suggested pleasantly.

"That's just the point. I wanted everything shipshape for when he arrives. You're the only blot in our bank, Mrs Hocken. Now, if you could promise me a large cheque before next Friday, we'd all be smiling, wouldn't we?"

"I'll see what I can do," I promised, knowing I hadn't a cat in hell's chance of providing him with a cheque, however large or small, by next Friday.

"How did it go?" Don asked cheerfully the moment I walked in the back door.

"I think I'd rather not talk about it, petal. Is there a cup of tea?"

"Just mashed. I'll tell you what, I've a free hour this afternoon — shall we go shopping? That'll cheer you up a bit, won't it?"

"As long as we don't spend any money at it," I groaned.

"We won't go into Stapleford . . ." Don tried to keep a cheery face. "We'll go somewhere else."

I have wished a million times that I had refused, but I didn't. I got into the car and off we went.

"Is there a pet shop in this area?" I asked Don. "I've just remembered, we've run out of chew bars at home."

"Yes, there's a big one. Don't you remember? Round the corner."

I normally buy all my pet food supplies from the local shop in Sandiacre. I patronise this particular one, as live animals are never sold there. There is nothing guaranteed to upset me more than seeing pets shut up in little cages. If only I had known the misery and heartache going into that new pet shop was to bring me, I would have run screaming in the opposite direction. As soon as we entered the shop, we spotted her. She was crammed into a cage far too small.

"Look at that poor dog."

Don immediately walked over to the pen. "Doesn't look like a puppy to me."

She had long, spindly legs, with a tail to match, a nose that was reminiscent of Concorde and ears that stuck out from the side of her head like bats' wings.

An assistant came to the pen. "Do you like her?" she asked. "She came in today. Very cheap. We're only asking five pounds for her, seeing as she's the last in the litter."

"What is she?" I had never seen anything quite like it before. I could only describe her colour as khaki. Her coat was fine and lay close to her body.

"We're not really sure what she is." The girl smiled. "A cross between something or other."

"How old is she? Surely she's not a puppy?" I asked.

"Only fourteen weeks."

"Good grief, she'll grow to the size of a Great Dane at that rate," Don said, as he poked his fingers through the wire.

She looked up at us in a knowing sort of way. She knew we were daft enough to take her home. Don paid over the five-pound note and lifted her from the pen. She was roughly the size of an adult Labrador.

"I don't think I can carry her all the way to the car."

The assistant, who was obviously only too keen to see the back of this dog, offered to lend us a collar and lead. Out on the pavement, our new possession sat and refused to move an inch. She pointed her nose into the air and stared at me with cold, blue eyes that sent shivers down my spine. Don clicked at her and gave a friendly tug on the lead.

"Here, let me have a go." I took some chocolate drops out of my pocket. "C'mon, this way," I said, offering her a chocolate drop. She sniffed it and declined the offer.

We tried gentle persuasion, cajoling her, tugging her gently, patting our legs, all to no avail. We then tried brute force.

"You pull, I'll push," I instructed Don.

After a few feet of this, we realized she'd wear her bottom out before we reached the car park.

"You'll have to carry her," I told Don. "There's nothing else for it."

I decided to call her Elsa. A very pretty name for a very ugly dog. As soon as Don had put Elsa into the back of our car and closed the door, the noise began. She screeched like a braking car.

"Quiet Elsa, we won't be long." I don't think she heard me over the din she was making.

Don sat behind the steering wheel. "I can't drive home with that noise."

"I'll get in the back," I told him. "I can stroke her through the dog guard. That might calm her down a bit. Elsa, be quiet, there's a good girl." I fondled her ears. She continued screeching. "No!" I said in a firmer voice. "That will not do. Now be quiet."

I'm afraid Don did have to drive home with that noise because nothing I could do or say would stop her. On reaching home, all hell broke loose. She didn't like the other dogs and made it quite plain that if any of them came within three feet of her, they would suffer the consequences.

CHAPTER SIX

ELSA'S INFLUENCE

Life was never the same after Elsa. Every living thing in the house suffered her presence and changed because of her. Our dogs had never lived as a pack. Don and I had always been the leaders and, so far, there had been no challenge from them . . . until Elsa, who systematically worked her way through the dogs, deciding who she could master and who she couldn't. Their first meeting in the garden was an education to anyone who is interested in dog behaviour. The moment Elsa approached Katy and Mocha they gave in, showing obvious fear of her, rolling on their backs and putting their feet in the air. After achieving this act of submission, Elsa went on to Buttons and Bracken, who did their very best to pretend that she didn't exist at all. They both sat together, backs pressed up against the wall as Elsa approached them, turning their heads away from her, afraid to look into her face. She decided they were a pushover and went over to Teak.

Teak stood stock still with a disgusted expression on her face, while Elsa stalked round her. She was not afraid to look this strange dog in the eye. After a few minutes of Elsa's aggressive behaviour, Teak took action, emitting a deep-throated growl. Don and I stood quietly by, at the ready in case any fights broke out. To our relief, Elsa submitted, but not in the normal manner. She just backed off. She was incredibly cunning for, realizing that she wouldn't get the better of Teak, she followed close behind her, waiting for a moment of inattention on Teak's part and then I felt sure she would attack. But Teak was too alert and quick witted for Elsa.

"Do you think you can train her?" Don threw out the challenge.

I'm far too egotistical to admit that I couldn't train a dog. "Of course I can. I shall have her entered in the obedience shows by the summer," I assured him, though I didn't feel the least bit confident about this dog's training.

My first problem was house-training but that would be easy. Hadn't I taught Katy so quickly a year ago? There's nothing like the present, I told myself, and walked round the garden with Elsa, repeating, "Busy dog . . . busy dog." After three quarters of an hour Elsa was a busy dog so I felt quite happy to let her in the dog room. Nobody wanted this ugly looking creature sharing their bed. The dog room has three dog beds. Katy and Mocha took one, Buttons and Teak the other. Bracken, of course, was in the lounge on the settee. Elsa was left to the large dog bed in the corner. She didn't like that. She stalked up and down, whining.

"Quiet!" I told her. "Get on your bed." I took her to the bed and patted it. She stared at me with cold, blue eyes and I knew she had no intention whatsoever of getting on that bed. I lifted her — no mean feat for a dog her size. "On your bed," I said again as I placed her gently down. "Good girl."

The moment I let her go, she was off the bed and whining again. I spent twenty minutes repeating this over and over again. This dog was not going to get the better of me. She did. I gave in. I walked out of the dog room and closed the door behind me in the hope that she would settle down. But the whining continued until it reached car brakes pitch again.

"Is there any tea?" Don asked, as he came in from the surgery.

"You'll have to wait until I've quietened this dog down," I said. I went back in the dog room. "I've had enough of this, Elsa. Now just be quiet."

There was a huge puddle on the floor. Well, I could hardly blame her. Perhaps that's what she'd been whining for. I took her outside into the garden. "Busy dog," I told her.

I had no time now to stand outside in the garden with Elsa so I closed the back door while I prepared Don's tea. Only thirty seconds elapsed before the whining began.

"You'll have to let her in," Don said. "You can't have that noise outside."

"Just watch your toast then," I replied. "I'll have to go out in the garden with her. It's no good leaving it to chance, is it?"

That evening at eight o'clock, when the dogs were allowed through into the lounge, I was unable to sit down and relax, as Don and I normally did, just enjoying the company of each other and our dogs. Elsa had to be watched. I wasn't over-keen on soggy carpets. Unlike the other dogs, Elsa would not lie down. She paced up and down the hall. I paced with her, into the kitchen, round the lounge. She tried going upstairs, to which I told her immediately that the upstairs portion of our house was definitely out of bounds. I presented her with squeaky toys, rubber bones and chew bars to try and channel her energy. She refused all. At ten-thirty I was exhausted. I sat down in my usual chair.

"Where's Elsa?" Don asked immediately.

"She's in the hall, lying down. I think she's going to sleep at long last."

"Are you sure Elsa's all right?" Don asked me at eleven o'clock. "She's very quiet."

"Well, she has to sleep sometime," I told him, "but I'll check." I heaved myself out of the chair and walked into the hall. Elsa was still lying in the place I'd left her but there was a foot square of hall carpet bald. She had prised out each individual tuft and eaten it. There was no sign of loose carpet anywhere. Chewed carpet I can understand but plucked carpet amazed me. It had obviously taken a lot of care and patience to pluck the individual tufts out and leave the canvas unscathed.

I admonished her and brought her into the lounge, where I could keep an eye on her. She stalked up to the settee and stared at Katy. Poor little Katy had curled herself up in a corner, next to Teak. I thought she was fast asleep, but the approach of Elsa brought her instantly alert. She leaped off the settee and ran to my chair. Elsa immediately took up the vacant place on the settee.

Mocha had been sitting by the bookcase, staring at the wall-light, when she shook herself, pottered about and decided that she, too, wanted a place on the coveted settee. If Elsa had growled at Mocha, I could have told her off. But she didn't. She just lay there and stared at her. Mocha backed off a couple of paces in bewilderment, then she turned herself round, pressing her rear end to the cushion. First, she raised one back leg onto the settee and stood for a moment, waiting, no doubt, to see if there were any repercussions from Elsa. There was silence. She slowly and quietly hitched the other back leg onto the settee. There she remained, for a full five minutes, her front paws and nose touching the carpet. Don and I watched in fascinated silence. Then slowly and carefully, she insinuated her body onto the settee. It took fifteen minutes before the last paw left the floor. She gave a little sigh of achievement before fixing her gaze on the curtain rail. Elsa was crushed, half of her body underneath Mocha, the other half jammed over the settee arm.

"Would you credit that?" Don commented, placing his half-empty mug on the coffee table. He'd always protected his beer well since the night of Katy's orgy.

"Yes. Mocha views Elsa as Medusa. As long as she doesn't get eye contact, she's safe."

"Can't you tell her off quietly?" I mumbled over my cup of tea the next morning. I was still half-asleep.

"I've tried that," Don told me, in no uncertain terms. "It doesn't work."

"Well, shouting at her obviously isn't working, is it?" I'm always in a very argumentative mood at eight o'clock in the morning. I walked like a zombie into the dog room and pointed a finger at Elsa. "Be quiet, for goodness' sake!"

The other dogs sat around looking at me with bemused expressions on their faces, except for Katy, who was trying desperately to hide under the blanket in the far dog bed.

"Oh, poor Katy. I'm not shouting at you." I knelt down to stroke and reassure her. This was the signal for Elsa to leap on my back and prod her sharp, hard nose into my neck.

It was at that moment I realized that I had met a dog, for the first time in my life, I didn't like. I knew I was never going to like her. That knowledge made me feel excessively guilty. Elsa was our responsibility. We had brought her home and we must do our best for her. I resolved that however I felt towards this dog, I must try not to show it. Somewhere she must have attributes. I'd find them and make the best use of them.

"Elsa, sit!" I commanded. I was embarking on her training. I eased her back, with my right hand on her collar, and pushed gently down with my left, near her rump. She turned round and stared at me, while resisting the gentle persuasion. Her expression said it all: Go to hell!

I hate using force with a dog. It only makes them turn against training. It's much easier to persuade them, if you can, but I was finding it very difficult to persuade Elsa. I tried another tack. Holding a titbit high up, I tried to get her to back off for it, into a sit position. She took one look at the titbit, snorted, as if to say, It's no good bribing me with food, and stood staring at me.

With a young puppy, the gentlest touch on the bottom will bring her into a sit. Elsa was huge, enormously strong, leggy and very fast. If she thought, for one moment, I was forcing her to do something, she would rebel against it. I stroked her, talked to her gently, moved my left hand slowly down her back and tried again. It worked. She'd relaxed herself into a sit. I leaped about with great excitement.

"What a clever girl!" I said. "You are a super dog."

I took a squeaky toy from my pocket and threw it for her. No response. I got the impression she felt herself above doing stupid things like chasing squeaky toys, but I'd succeeded in my first lesson. If she wouldn't play with squeaky toys and she wasn't interested in titbits, I had to find a way round it. It would have been easy to use pure and simple force, but that isn't my method. I found it much easier to get her interested in titbits by having another dog with me and constantly offering titbits to the other dog. Eventually, Elsa gave in and accepted her titbit . . . only out of jealousy, but it did work.

The methods I had used with Katy were totally useless with Elsa, and I began to feel very incompetent as a dog trainer. I tried every way I could to get Elsa to come to me when I called her, from offering a titbit to waving toys and knotted tights about, to jumping up and down in the air, clapping my hands and shouting with excitement, to rolling on the floor laughing. Nothing had any effect. She would stand at the top of the garden and just look down her nose at me.

Don popped his head out of the surgery window during one of my efforts to get Elsa to respond. "What are you doing rolling on the grass giggling to yourself?" he asked. "People would think you're mad, if they saw you."

"I'm trying to get Elsa to come," I replied.

He glanced across at her. She stood, stock still. "I don't think you're going to succeed," he said, almost to himself.

"No, neither do I," I said, as I stood up and brushed the grass from my clothes.

I tried the long lead method, putting her on it, letting her out in the garden and calling her in. She wouldn't come, of course, unless I physically forced her by hauling on the end of the lead. I didn't like doing this but it was the only way. When she reached me, I gave her lots of fuss, a titbit and let her go out again on the lead. I didn't feel at all confident that she would respond and return to me in the park, and I was extremely stupid, therefore, to let her off there.

"She's bound to come back," I told Don, "especially with all the other dogs." But she didn't. Don and I raced off after her. Not a lot of good when you compared her deer-like speed to our out-of-breath staggers. Each time we neared her, she ducked and fled off like a khaki shadow into the distance. "Don't panic," I said to Don, as I felt the terror rising inside me of losing a dog.

"Look . . ." Don puffed, "this isn't going to get us anywhere. Let's go to the middle of the park and play with the other dogs. I think she'll be so annoyed we're ignoring her that she'll come back."

It was a good idea. For fifteen minutes we threw the retrieve, played with the dogs and talked to them, and gradually Elsa came nearer. She would never play retrieves. Her idea of a game was disruptive. She'd circle all the dogs, darting in here and there with a snap and darting out again. The other dogs did their utmost to ignore her and put up a good show of pretending that Elsa was nothing to do with them. I only wished I could do the same.

The only one of us, canine or human, who got on well with Elsa was Kerensa. Elsa was a contrary creature, fighting for dominance over adults and dogs and yet accepting Kerensa as a friend. They would play in the back garden for hours.

I never quite trusted Elsa and was popping out every five minutes to make sure all was well. Kerensa was quite adamant about her ability to control this peculiar animal.

"Don't worry, Mummy. We're having a marvellous game."

She had Elsa on a collar and lead, walking her up and down the garden. The dog was quite happy to comply. "You won't pull her about or anything, will you?"

Kerensa stopped walking and looked at me with accusing grey eyes.

"No, of course you won't. But what I mean is if she starts being at all funny with you, you will call me, won't you?"

She nodded. I left the back door open, still feeling a little bit jittery.

But even Kerensa soon went off Elsa. She was the proverbial spanner in the works. She ruined everything. At home, there was no peace from her whining. In the park, the dogs were unable to play without her interfering. None of them liked her and it was obvious they were trying, every way they knew how, to tell me. When Elsa rushed at Bracken, he dived behind my legs for protection and pressed his body into the back of my knees until I almost fell over.

"Bracken, what are you doing, you silly boy? Go and fight back. Don't let her bully you."

He put his rose-petal ears on and looked at me with a pleading expression. He might not be able to speak, but his eyes said volumes.

Elsa had as much difficulty working out Mocha's mental capacity as I did. She would prod her with that long, thin nose. Mocha wouldn't budge. Then the evil dog would bite Mocha's ear. Poor little Mocha would squeak with terror while her front feet marched up and down on the spot. She looked like a grape treader.

"Go on, Mocha, bite her back!"

Mocha sat down again and stared at me, her eyes holding as much expression as a blank television screen.

Elsa, deciding Mocha was no fun as a target, turned on Katy. That's when I managed to grab her collar. Inside, I was fuming and I stood silently, trying to control my temper. I knew the worst thing I could do at this point was to tell Elsa off for not coming when she was called. Theoretically I should have praised her, lavishly, but I couldn't. I put her on the lead and marched her back to the car.

CHAPTER SEVEN

THE BEGINNING OF THE END

I stared despondently into my pan of gravy. It had happened again. After sixteen years of daily practice making gravy, I still couldn't succeed. Tracey automatically handed me the whisk.

"How did you know?" I asked her, grudgingly.

"I've never seen you make a pan of gravy yet that hadn't got lumps in it," she laughed.

It's difficult enough to admit to myself that I'm useless at gravy-making, but when other people find out, it's humiliating. Apart from the sound of my whisk, all was peaceful. A rarity in our home. Elsa was in the garden pottering about and, as she was silent, I willingly left her to it.

"There you are, Tracey." I handed her the dirty whisk. "I should wash it now before it gets chance to set."

The whisking process didn't exactly disintegrate the lumps in my gravy, but acted more as a magnet. The whisk always came out of the pan with large lumps clinging to it.

"Why do I always get the dirty jobs?" Tracey grumbled. She scrubbed and scraped at the whisk. In the middle of her cleaning-up operation, she stopped and stared out of the window. "Have you seen Elsa?" she asked.

"No. And while all is quiet, I don't think I want to."

"I feel you ought to go and have a look outside," Tracey said in a serious voice. "That dog's covered in soil."

Don had spent every minute of his spare time over the last two months building us a patio and I had suffered the anguish with him of slab-laying, wall-building and shrub-planting and, now it was finished, even I had to admit it was a masterpiece. He'd built a raised garden in the middle so the dogs wouldn't climb all over his plants. Other trees were placed around in large pots and Don had prided himself that not only did it look magnificent, but it was completely dog-proof. When I say he was proud of it, it would be more truthful to say that he was obsessed by it, shooting out from the surgery every few minutes to make sure that nothing had been disturbed. If the wind had blown a crumb of soil off the garden, he replaced it with loving care. And if one of the dogs even looked as if they were sniffing one of the plant pots or a piece of wall, Don would be seen rushing from the surgery, threatening them with violence.

"Oh no!" I groaned. "Oh please . . . no." I buried my face in my hands. "I daren't look, Tracey. I just couldn't bear it. Go out and tell me it's not true. She hasn't touched the patio. She hasn't, has she?" I yelled after Tracey as she opened the back door. "Just tell me that she hasn't been anywhere near it."

"*Elsa!* You horrible dog!" Tracey screamed. "How could you possibly have done all that damage?"

Much to my horror, she then started to laugh. "Don't laugh about it," I said, plucking up the courage to look outside the back door. "It's all right for you, isn't it? You can go home. I've got to live here with that dog and that patio."

"Have you seen what she's done to that tree?"

The tree, which was planted in the middle of the walled garden, had been beautiful. Now it lay, its roots exposed and its leaves flattened into the soil. The honeysuckle had been torn from its pot and shredded. What had been a beautiful border of pansies was now floating up the garden like confetti.

"Quick!" I yelled to Tracey. "Don'll be home in a minute. Help me get it back."

Tracey stood, helpless. "You can't put it back. It's had it," she said.

"Don't be a pessimist. Look, pull that tree out of the soil. I'll get the roots back in." I carefully dug a hole and re-buried the roots, trying to get the tree to stand upright again. I managed it, after banking the soil high on one side for support. "Sweep all those petals up, quick. And that honeysuckle . . . put it in the dustbin." I began removing the tree's telltale leaves from the soil. "If only we had more time," I said, "I could glue those leaves back on." I didn't share Tracey's amusement, not one little bit.

"You can't glue leaves back on."

"Yes I could," I told her, "given the time."

At that moment, I heard the crunch of wheels on the driveway and smelt the potatoes burning. I was almost in tears as Don walked through the gate.

"It's not my fault," I said. "It's that horrible dog. Everything's gone wrong in this house since she came. I burnt the potatoes because of her."

Don has a much calmer, more placid temperament than I have. Apart from mumbling something about Elsa, he ignored the patio whereas I had got to fever pitch over it. If there's one thing that I can grumble about, living with Don, it's that he seems so perfect, and I am not. He can handle any situation with calm resolution, while I get sick with panic.

I sat watching him eat his potato-less dinner. "Sorry," I told him.

"It's not your fault." He leaned over and gave me a gravy kiss on the cheek.

I wiped the lumps of gravy away and stood up. "That's it!" I said, "I'm taking Elsa out. I'm going to train that dog if it's the last thing I do."

I fetched her from the dog room, determined that this time I would take her out alone and concentrate on her training. All the other dogs sat back and looked at me with hopeful expressions. Little Katy beat her tail against the wooden bed and flapped her huge ears backwards and forwards in anticipation. I was so tempted to leave Elsa at home and take the rest, but I knew where my duty lay.

I confess, I'd rather run the gauntlet than take Elsa for a walk. She was a liability, even on the lead. She seemed to have as much sensitivity around the neck as a brick wall. She'd walk quite nicely for a few steps and then hurl herself, with great force, at the end of the lead. Every second of the walk, I was tensed up, ready for the lunges. A second's inattention on my part would have me lunging after her. It wasn't so much the pulling of the lead that was embarrassing, as the noise. She hated other dogs. The problem was I couldn't see other dogs coming soon enough to take avoiding action. I would only know of their presence in the immediate vicinity by Elsa's screams. Any passer-by would instantly stop and look across at me accusingly, thinking I was trying to murder her. The screech she put on when she saw another dog sounded like the squeals of a trapped pig. I had to fight an overwhelming urge to run home. Instead, I doubled my determination and took her on to the local park for intensive training.

I was now beginning to understand the other side of dog-ownership. I'd never had any sympathy for all those people I'd met in the past who had been unable to cope with their dogs. It was all their fault, I told myself. Lack of training and understanding on the owner's part, I was convinced, was always the problem. Perhaps, in the future, I would listen with a more sympathetic ear.

Heel work, recalls, stays . . . we went through them all, but it wasn't much fun, especially when passing dog owners stopped to give me their advice. I had to quell a violent urge to strangle them. If only Elsa was like Katy. Katy, who loved to work. Whose tail thrashed nineteen to the dozen if I mentioned heel work. Who was a pleasure to take out for a walk. Elsa was the complete reverse. She hated working. She glared at me with those pale blue eyes every time I gave a command, and the fuss and praise I gave her was not reciprocated. I'd given up trying to play with her. You feel stupid throwing squeaky toys and having to fetch them yourself all the time. I knew it was my fault.

I spent those days alternating between disliking Elsa and disliking myself. If only I could have found a little affection for her in my heart, things would have been different. But I resented her. I resented the burnt potatoes and the destroyed patio, the holes in the carpet and the noise. Above all, I resented the noise.

CHAPTER EIGHT

TEAK'S CHRISTMAS

I had a feeling that soon Elsa would attack, not one of us, but one of the dogs, and I was convinced that Teak would be her first target. At night, Bracken slept on the settee. The rest of the dogs were confined to the dog room. Every night, when I went to bed, I lay awake worrying and listening. I could feel the air charged, like a storm approaching, and I imagined scenes of horror in the dog room.

It was a few days before Christmas when I voiced my fears to Don. Yes, he confirmed, he'd thought exactly the same thing. We both agreed that if anybody was in danger during the night, it was Teak. So Teak was to sleep in the lounge with Bracken, out of harm's way. The very first night that Teak slept with Bracken, I awoke with a start at about three o'clock in the morning. Kerensa was shaking me.

"Mummy, I can hear something in the kitchen. I can hear paper crackling and things moving about."

It normally takes me at least two hours and six cups of tea to come round, but the shock of Kerensa telling me we were being burgled woke me up quicker than being dipped into an icy bath. I ran downstairs, never giving a thought to what I would do if a big hefty burglar was raiding our kitchen. I threw all the lights on and, as I entered the kitchen, I spotted our burglar. It was a brown one with four legs, called Teak.

She had somehow managed to open the kitchen cupboard where I had put the Christmas hamper I had been saving all the year for. Teak was halfway through a strawberry jelly. Remnants of Dundee cake and cream crackers lay around the kitchen floor.

My first instinct was to sit among the debris and weep. I am not normally like that but I have to admit that Elsa was getting me down, making me feel bad tempered and I really am not myself at three o'clock in the morning. But Kerensa and Teak saved me from total despair. Kerensa put her head round the kitchen door gingerly, to see Teak sitting in the corner, pawing at her mouth and yawning. She had strawberry jelly stuck all round her teeth. Kerensa began to giggle and it was infectious.

After cleaning up the kitchen floor and reprimanding the still wide-mouthed Teak, I crept back to bed. Don had slept through it all.

The next night, I firmly closed the kitchen door and hoped I would have an undisturbed night. It had been Kerensa'a birthday and the party had been packed with over-exuberant children. I was exhausted. I slept like a log. The next morning nothing seemed disturbed. Teak and Bracken were waiting at the bottom of the stairs to greet me. I let all the dogs out into the garden and had my usual two cups of tea. It wasn't till walk-time came and I was putting a collar and lead on Teak that I noticed something odd about her. Her stomach seemed swollen and distended. I had a feel around. It was as solid as a rock.

"Teak, what's the matter with you?" I asked her. I received her usual response: she bounced up and down and hit me with her nose. Despite the fact that I knew the kitchen door had been closed, I went to look in the cupboard. The remains of our hamper were still intact.

"Mummy!" Kerensa called from the dining room. "Where did you put my birthday cake?"

"It's on the tea trolley," I called back, "covered up with some grease-proof paper."

"No, it isn't."

I went to look for myself. There, near the tea trolley, lay the grease-proof paper, shredded, on the floor. All that was left of Kerensa's cake was the silver board it had stood on and a few green trees and candles. Every crumb had disappeared. Kerensa was so upset. It had been a beautiful birthday cake in the shape of a stable, with Smarties for the roof, and only a small portion had been cut away for the children the day before. It would have lasted for months. Teak had crept into the dining room during the night and gorged herself on Kerensa's birthday cake.

Teak spent most of that day writhing on her bed, intermittent groans coming from her overfed body. She never stirred at dog-feeding time. Although Teak was directly to blame for eating the cake and half of the Christmas hamper, it was really Elsa's fault. If it hadn't been for Elsa, Teak would never have had the opportunity to eat all the food.

The next night, 23 December, I was extra careful to ensure that all the doors were closed, except for the lounge. There was nothing, I told myself as I climbed the stairs, that Teak could possibly eat tonight. I had ensured everything was well out of her reach. Oh, how wrong I was!

The next morning, I didn't even get the whole way down the stairs before I noticed the hall carpet had bits of paper all over it. I picked them up and tried to piece them together. What were they off? Where had they come from? And then I noticed my bag, a large leather one that hangs in the hall. I had it specially made a few years ago, a shoulder-bag that I could throw everything into with a beautiful painting of Emma on the front. Now there was a large hole chewed in the bottom. I had left the dogs' Christmas presents in it the day before — chocolate drops, chew bars and Bonios. Teak had eaten them all.

Bracken came from the lounge with his rose-petal expression on, slowly wagging his tail and shuffling his back legs along the carpet. A sure sign that he felt guilty, even if he wasn't. He nuzzled round me, hoping for forgiveness.

"Well, you didn't do it, Bracken, you're a good boy."

I put my head into the lounge and saw yet more paper on the floor, coloured silver paper. "How stupid can you get?" I said out loud. I'd put chocolate decorations on the top of the Christmas tree . . . little chocolate Santa Clauses for Kerensa. They'd been eaten. Removed delicately, but nevertheless eaten.

Christmas Eve must be the most uncomfortable night Don and I have ever had. To leave Teak and Kerensa's Christmas presents in the lounge was just asking for trouble. There was no option. Teak had to come to bed with us. I am sure she thought sleeping on our bed for the night was her Christmas present. She rolled in ecstasy, dug the quilt round her, snored, groaned, kicked out with all four paws until we were both left with no blankets and hardly any bed room.

Teak sprang out of bed on Christmas morning, full of doggy joy. Don and I crept wearily out of the bit of bed that had been left to us, feeling as if we had been galloped over by a herd of Teaks.

In the New Year, I forced myself to take Elsa to the dog training club. I had found a nice one a little distance away from where I lived, but it was worth the travelling. All the people were friendly and their training techniques were excellent. Katy and I had been going for a few months. It was our special evening and we really enjoyed it, but I knew that if I wanted to get Elsa trained I had to take her along too. Poor little Katy, she was so upset. None of the old tail-wagging and bouncing around when she saw Elsa standing at the front door.

When I arrived at the club, everyone was astonished.

"What's that? It certainly isn't a Labrador," they all chorused.

Everyone associates me with Labradors. If I go out alone, no-one recognizes me. If I'm accompanied by a Labrador, I get stopped in the street.

Katy, who normally greeted dogs and owners alike, crept under a chair and refused to budge. To put it mildly, Elsa was a pain. Admittedly, she ignored most of the dogs . . . except the Labradors, which she tried to lunge at. That told me a lot. She might live with four Labradors, but she hated them.

With the help and patience of the trainer and other dog owners, I did get Elsa to behave, but it was a sheer battle of wills. It wasn't until the end of the evening that I remembered Katy, still huddled under the chair in the corner. The trainer's anorak had been thrown over the back of the chair and as she put it on, Katy crept out, looking extremely guilty . . . and no wonder. The anorak had one of its sleeves missing. There were just a few chewed ends left at the shoulder seam. Katy, out of sheer worry and frustration, had chewed her way up the sleeve during the evening. I couldn't blame her, poor little dog. She was getting nearly as neurotic as me.

CHAPTER NINE

GOODBYE ELSA

The situation with Elsa went from bad to worse. We had taken Teak out of the dog room and now I was worrying about Katy. Katy, whose sweet little nature and trusting ways were beginning to change. She was afraid of men. Don had told me that on the walks she refused to go anywhere near him and I could see she was nervous of him in the house.

"What have you done?" I asked him. I knew that Katy was well behaved out on the walks and Don would have no reason to reprimand her.

"I can't think," he replied. "I'm always offering her titbits, but she is afraid of me."

It took me a while to work out that Don's scoldings of Elsa were rubbing off on Katy. At the dog shows, Katy was losing places if the judge was a man. She would do anything but go near him.

"Take Katy out of the dog room," Don suggested. "Don't put her in there in the day or the night and then she won't feel threatened."

It had been a long time since a dog had slept in the bedroom with us — apart from that awful night with Teak and those few nights we had tried with Bracken — and I still missed the sound of Emma's deep breathing during the night and her delight when the alarm went off in the morning. She would jump on the bed and nuzzle her nose into the sheets. In the small hours of the morning, I had often lain awake listening, hoping for the sounds of a dog and missing Emma. Now I decided that Katy would go to bed with us. I slept a lot easier, not only being able to listen again to those reassuring sounds of a dog asleep, but also knowing that Katy was safe from Elsa. It was not long before Buttons, too, had to be taken from the dog room at night for her own safety.

One afternoon, when all the dogs were out in the garden waiting for their dinner, I heard a shriek of sheer terror. I dashed out to see Elsa shaking Buttons by the throat. Buttons is a huge Labrador, shaped more like a bull than a dog. Elsa, although she was tall, was long and thin and didn't look as if she had enough strength to pick Katy up, let alone Buttons. I could only assume her strength came from hatred. I grabbed Elsa by the back of her neck and shook her. The shock made her release Buttons, who immediately crept off, tail and belly low to the ground. She tried to hide herself in the corner of the garden. It was the first time I had ever seen Buttons afraid of anything and my sympathy went out to her.

I, too, was afraid of Elsa. Not in the same way that Buttons feared her, but I felt that Elsa was ruining our lives. My nerves were in shreds and I'd snapped at Don and Kerensa a hundred times over the last few months. Don and I never normally exchange a cross word. We just don't argue. We are so much alike that we think and do alike. He could so easily have turned on me and blamed me for bringing Elsa home, but I knew his feelings were as mine . . . that she was our responsibility. But there comes a time when people must be considered before dogs and I was afraid that Elsa was driving Don and I apart. Normally so placid, so understanding and even tempered, even Don was becoming a little frayed at the edges.

Once I had made the decision that Elsa had to go, I breathed a big sigh of relief. I felt terribly guilty and inadequate that I had failed her, but that made me more determined to find her the right home. I placed adverts in every paper, hoping for a large response so that I could sift through prospective owners. Many callers were deterred by my total honesty. I realized it was pointless not to tell the truth about her. Although there was no love lost between us, I couldn't bear the thought of her ending up in an animal shelter.

Mrs Markham had passed the test on the telephone. She had no other dogs and, as her husband was away most of the time, she wanted a large dog for protection as well as companionship. She came round almost immediately to meet Elsa. As I opened the door to her, I had my fingers crossed. To my utter amazement, they liked each other on sight. Mrs Markham sat in the lounge, her arms around Elsa, who was gently nuzzling her ears and licking her chin. That couldn't be my dog, I thought. She'd never sat quietly and shown gentle affection before.

For half an hour, I told Mrs Markham everything that had happened between us and why Elsa had to go. That dog knew every word I said. She flashed those cold, blue eyes at me with something I can only describe as akin to hatred.

"I'll take her," Mrs Markham said, after listening to all my derogatory remarks. I escorted them down the drive and watched as she encouraged Elsa into the back of her car. The dog jumped in, curled up, closed her eyes and breathed a large sigh of relief. It dawned on me, at that moment, that Elsa had been very unhappy living with us. She did not like sharing her home with other dogs. She didn't fit in with our routine. The plain truth of the matter was she didn't like us.

Even with those thoughts in my mind, as I walked back up the drive, I couldn't help a lump sticking in my throat and one or two tears running down my cheeks.

*

Our lives gradually got back to normality and peaceful harmony.

The next morning, everyone was light-hearted . . . the humans and the dogs.

"Now that Elsa's gone . . ." Kerensa looked at me earnestly. ". . . Can I bring Holly in?"

Holly, Ming, Rahni and Zimba lived in their cat house at the top of the garden. Originally, I put them there for safety, but now Kerensa was older and she realized that letting the cats out was dangerous. Over the past few months, she had formed a very deep relationship with Holly. They really loved each other. In fact, Holly loved Kerensa far more than she ever loved me. If I ever tried to administer a tablet to Holly or clip her claws, she would bite me. Kerensa could do anything with her.

Zimba and Rahni were happy outside. Rahni seemed to suffer from claustrophobia, and when she was brought in the house she would spend hours crying at the back door to be let back into her run. Zimba couldn't come in the house because I just couldn't trust him. He wasn't a friendly cat, he didn't like strangers and he wasn't keen on Kerensa. But Ming and Holly could live in the house happily, as long as nobody left the door open.

Holly became Kerensa's constant companion. She even took her to bed and Holly loved it. When I went out into the garden to train the dogs, Kerensa announced that she was going to train Holly.

I laughed. "You can't train cats, Kerensa. They're not at all like dogs, you know."

"Oh yes I can. You wait and see."

I left her to it, thinking she would soon realize Holly would not be as biddable as Bicky, her dog on wheels. About a week later, Kerensa marched in the kitchen and placed Holly on the stool.

"Watch this," she told me, her eyes gleeful.

She touched Holly gently near the tail and gave her the sit command. Holly sat. I laughed.

"Yes, Kerensa, but most cats will sit on a stool."

"Wait a minute," she said, impatiently, "you haven't seen it all yet."

She gave Holly a stroke. "Holly, stand!" Holly stood, tail waving in the air. Kerensa tapped the stool and gave Holly the command "Down!" Holly did it. I stood, open-mouthed in astonishment.

"You can't train cats," I told Kerensa.

She picked Holly up and cuddled her and carried her off into the lounge, without a word.

I saw Elsa three months later. She was an entirely different dog, relaxed, calm and friendly. The change was incredible.

CHAPTER TEN

MY LEFT EYE

After the successful operation I had in 1975 on the right eye, I always hoped that one day the same would happen with my left eye. Mr Shearing had said as much, so I was eager to go into hospital for another operation. One eye was fantastic . . . what would two eyes be like? I knew they wouldn't run in unison like everyone else's do. They would have a tendency to wander in different directions, but I didn't mind that. I couldn't use two at once but I could certainly use one at once. That meant I'd have a spare! I looked forward to the operation on my left eye with great excitement. After all, it should be a success. The right one had been, and maybe it would be even better than the right one.

It took me a long time to learn how restricting the vision I had actually was, because, having been blind for so many years, just a tiny bit of sight was everything to me. Being able to perceive colours and shapes and sunshine fooled me into thinking I had perfect sight. I remember the first week I came out of hospital. I was all for learning to drive a car, until I discovered that I couldn't see a vehicle at twenty-five yards, let alone a numberplate. I don't have distance or detailed vision and I can't see at all in the dark. Getting around is fine, as long as there is nothing untoward, like a hole in the pavement. Most of the time I can see obstacles like bikes and prams and people, but sometimes I seem to miss them, probably because my field of vision is so restricted and I can only look at a tiny part of the visual picture at once. So there are occasions when I walk into people, or fall over bikes. So what? It doesn't bother me.

The only thing that does bother me is the road. We live on a very busy main road and I am convinced that I shall end my days between tyre and tarmac. I am very careful. After all, I still have an acute pair of ears. The only problem is that human beings are very much visual animals and the vision side tends to overrule all the other senses of the body. When I go out to cross our busy main road, I look and listen and I am often sure there is nothing coming. I probably ignore the hearing sense that tells me there's a car racing up the road, and I run . . . I always run across the road. I feel that it would be much harder for the cars to hit a racing target. I have been so close to being run over that the cars have actually brushed past my legs or caught my clothing and, in all honesty, I would love to give up crossing roads, but then that would be giving in and I must never do that. If I once let the fears of not being able to see enough take over, then I might as well sit at home and turn into a cabbage.

The left eye, I thought, might give me just enough sight to cross the road safely but, alas, it wasn't to be. Everything went wrong on the first operation. Not only did it not work, it was extremely painful and the anaesthetic made me sick. I'm still not quite sure what really happened over the anaesthetic, but when I came round in hospital I found myself on a drip and wearing an oxygen mask. If I'd been a little more conscious, I'm sure I would have panicked, but I wasn't so I just took it for granted and everybody told me I was fine after that. Apart from the fact that I lost half a stone over the next five days, all was well.

Mr Shearing took great pains to explain the difficulties on the left eye. The lens is like an onion, with layers and layers of transparent skin. In the cataracts that people suffer in old age, the lens has hardened, turning the layers of skin opaque. The hardening process makes it easy to remove the lens without damaging the rest of the eye. The lens is, of course, then replaced by glasses.

Mine were very different. Being young, the lens was soft and sticky, making it very difficult to remove. Mr Shearing explained that he was trying to take the middle part of the lens away, so as not to disturb the eye, but this created problems with bits of floating lens. I could imagine a slip of the hand and the whole eye had gone west. Mr Shearing pointed out that it was a real sticky mess in there and it would take him time to clear the debris of lens. As he so aptly described it, my left eye looked like something the dog had chewed up and spat out.

"I think we should have another try in a few days," he told me.

I was reluctant to undergo another operation, but what is a few days' pain and sickness compared with sight? So I agreed, but I didn't look forward to it. In fact, I approached it with fear and trepidation. Even the pre-med did nothing to quell my fears as they wheeled me down to the operating theatre for the second time in six days.

Thankfully, that operation had no after-effects at all and I began to hope. Memories of the first operation came back to me. When the bandages were removed that time, I was let into a world of brilliance, a world of beautiful colours. Perhaps, this time, it would be even better and I remember sitting, again, in the little dressings room, as the sister removed the pad from my left eye.

I was breathless with anticipation, waiting for that wonderful moment when colours and brilliance flood in. But there was nothing. Absolutely nothing at all. The left eye only opened onto blackness. It was with a sinking heart I returned to the ward this time. I told myself I should be extremely grateful, for I had one eye with sight. Restricted it might be, but it was wonderful and I knew only too well, from past experience, that I was very, very lucky to have one good eye. Most of my relatives had undergone operations that were totally unsuccessful.

I was determined not to stay for another operation, and when Mr Shearing came to see me even he admitted defeat — at least, for the time being.

"Sometime, in the future," he told me, "when you've got over the disappointment, we'll try again."

Perhaps, if I'd have known what would happen in the future, I would have stayed in that hospital and begged him to keep trying, but I didn't know that, soon after, Mr Shearing would have a heart attack which forced him into retirement. I know many people felt, as I did, that it was terrible that such a thing should happen to a man who had achieved so much. It was devastating to the profession and to his patients.

I decided to shelve the prospect of another operation. Now Mr Shearing was unable to do it, I didn't believe I would have faith in anyone else. Not only that, but I always felt just a little guilty about wanting more. Hadn't I had my fair share of miracles to last anyone else three lifetimes? I shouldn't be greedy. I had sight, I had Kerensa — a perfectly sighted daughter — and above all, and most important to me, I had Don. And the more I saw of my friends' and acquaintances' marriages breaking up around me, the more I appreciated finding Don.

Our marriage has been absolutely perfect. A lot of people really will not believe me when I tell them we don't argue. We have never argued. There is never a time when we are not speaking to each other, nor do we ever get short tempered and shout at each other. It just never happens. I think it has a lot to do with temperament and the fact that both of us appreciate the other's need for independence. I can go off at weekends to my dog shows without a grumble from Don, and I am the same when he wants to go out in the evening for a drink. I don't mind at all. I am quite happy to sit at home. I've been with some wives who have gone absolutely berserk at their husbands because they are half an hour late coming home from the pub. I worry if Don's late. I'm almost sick with terror that something could have happened to him, and I know he worries if I am late home from dog shows, but when he comes in the door, I don't yell and scream at him. I throw my arms around him and say, "Thank God you're all right."

I know that the key to a happy marriage is mutual respect, always treating each other politely and never taking your partner for granted. Despite the fact that we both work at home, I never get fed up with seeing Don. In fact, on a Friday, when he leaves the surgery and goes out visiting house-bound patients, I feel lonely and wish that he was in the surgery near to me.

CHAPTER ELEVEN

CONTACT LENSES

Neither of us likes leaving home for too long, so going away on holiday is a very rare occurrence. In fact, we really only do it for Kerensa's sake. It seems unfair that she should have to stay at home just because we want to. And then, of course, there are the dogs. Far too many to take away with us and we hate leaving some behind. We are very lucky to have a friend who will come and live in and look after the dogs. But the thought of going on holiday without any dogs at all is purgatory, so we have to find somewhere that will accept at least two . . . preferably three. Hotels are definitely out. Even if they allow dogs, they are only allowed in bedrooms and, for some unknown reason, hotels tend to have pale-coloured carpets and white bedspreads, which just do not go with three soggy dogs. And I know we are going to get soggy dogs when we go on holiday, because it always rains!

By chance, I saw an advert for a cottage just outside Ross-on-Wye: "Dogs most welcome." I wondered just how welcome as I dialled the telephone number at the bottom of the advert. I made tentative enquiries of the owner about price and vacancies and then I broached the dog situation.

"Do you really welcome dogs?" I asked.

"Yes, of course. In fact, we only let it to dog people."

I was shocked. "How many dogs can we bring?" I thought that would stop her in her tracks.

"As many as you like, I don't mind at all."

"Do you mean we could bring three?" I asked.

"Of course. You can bring six if you like."

I booked our holiday there and then. It was impossible to take all of the dogs because of room in the car and, if we wanted the house minding, we had to leave a couple at home for the company and protection of Mrs Tolley, who can be well trusted to look after house and hounds.

I had been so overwhelmed by the "dogs welcomed" bit that I hadn't thought much about the cottage and, as Don drove the car up the lonely lanes just outside Ross, I began to wonder. It said in the pamphlet there was a bathroom and a television and a large kitchen. If I knew anything of our luck, the bathroom meant a tin bath and one of those old pedestal sinks, and a loo behind the shed at the bottom of the garden. Well, never mind, I thought, you have to sacrifice something if you want to take the dogs with you.

We were all pleasantly surprised. The cottage was lovely and comfortable, with all mod cons and even a little paddock out the back for the dogs to run in. The only setback was the stove. It was electric and I'm used to gas and I felt, from the moment I walked into that holiday cottage kitchen, that the stove hated me. It knew I was a regular gas-user and was determined to get me for it. Its first little antic was to throw a plate at me. It had been switched off for ages and I casually put a dinner plate on the hob. It instantly threw it off, in tiny pieces. I'm not a bad cook, apart from gravy and custard, but that stove made me look like Ria, out of *Butterflies*. It wouldn't cook my Yorkshire pudding. It burnt the potatoes and it took me two hours to cook a plateful of chips. But I managed to ignore the stove and have nearly a week's enjoyable holiday.

Bracken, Katy and Ming proving it's much more
sensible to be a pet than a human

'Too many dogs'
lying on the front
lawn of our house

Teak on the beach at Weston-Super-Mare

Teak smiling for the camera

Pip Squeak at seven weeks

Three generations: *Left to right* Katy (grandma),
Psyche (mum) and baby Pip at three months

Mocha's last litter

Katy's babies

The scenery was fantastic in the Forest of Dene but as the week wore on my one and only good eye began to let me down. I really did think for a while that I had overused it in my eagerness to see everything. I felt as if I had a piece of sand lodged between my eye and the contact lens. Naturally, I repeatedly took the lens out and cleaned it in its soaking liquid. It didn't help. In fact, it made it worse. The sunlight — a very rare thing on our holidays, but there was plenty of it this time — was hurting my eyes. The last two days of our holiday I spent squinting around the place, looking through half-closed eyes at a very blurred picture.

As luck would have it, the weekend we arrived home was August Bank Holiday. Everybody was closed, including the doctors' surgery. I didn't feel it was that much of an emergency to go and trouble the hospital. I felt sure that my eye complaint, whatever it was, would pass and I'm a believer in the saying that if you ignore it long enough it will go away. I tried leaving the contact lens out but that made it even worse. It hurt every time I blinked or moved my eye. Initially, on putting the contact lens back in, it hurt like mad but then eased off after about fifteen minutes. So I had to sleep with my contact lens in. It was the only way I could get any sleep.

I had to suffer the Saturday night, the Sunday night and the Monday night before I could get in to see anyone at the doctors' and, again as luck would have it, it wasn't my usual GP. I explained my case to the doctor, who was sitting behind the desk, a dark blur. My eye now felt as if someone was sticking a knife in it and twisting it round every few seconds. The doctor had a cursory look, gave me a prescription and bid me good day. I dashed down to the chemist, ran home and put the ointment liberally into my aching, burning, eye. I spent Tuesday night awake. It was going from bad to worse. I was down at the Health Centre first thing, demanding to see my own doctor, who was now back

93

from his vacation. Sense at last. He didn't waste time looking at my eye, but referred me instantly to the eye consultant at the hospital.

It had been five years since my last visit and I had forgotten the idiocies of waiting-room procedure. There were hundreds of us along benches facing various directions. I sat and listened. I couldn't look any more, the light hurt too much.

"Mr Smedley, will you move up onto that bench over there? Mrs Smith, what are you doing down there? You're completely out of your place."

If I had not been in so much agony, I would have been in stitches with laughter. Everyone was shuffled here and there, it was like a silly board game. I wondered how the nurses kept tabs on everybody and how they managed to keep it all from ending up in one big muddle of who was to see who, and on what bench were which doctor's patients. I think I was there for two hours, in which time I daren't leave to go to the ladies', I daren't go and have a cup of tea in case I lost my place . . . and the agony was getting worse. And of course Mr Shearing was no longer there. I had to see a Mr Johnson, highly recommended by Mr Shearing, but not him.

I really felt I'd die of starvation, exposure and pain before I was allowed in. I'd been seen by two "under-doctors", shuffled from consulting room to consulting room, asked if I could read various numbers on the board. I couldn't even see the damn board. I hate the National Health Service's attitude towards most of their patients. They didn't believe I couldn't see any numbers on the board. They thought I was illiterate or stupid and constantly asked me if I could see this or that. The room was so dark that I wouldn't have been able to see anything with a pair of binoculars.

I fervently believe the National Health Service sets up a type of endurance course to try and weed out the weaker element. The rules of the game are simple. The first and most important one is that you must do exactly what you are told, without question. Sitting on uncomfortable wooden benches, hour after hour, without complaining. Submitting to endless house-doctors' probing and silly questions. Any attempt to argue with these doctors — such as telling them that you can't see the board and that you are not illiterate — is strictly against the rules. And failure to stay on your bench at all times, unless otherwise directed, no matter how desperate you may be to visit the toilet or seek liquid sustenance, will immediately forfeit your right to see the consultant that month. If you comply with all these rules and regulations, you get the star prize — one minute and thirty seconds with the consultant.

By the time I got in there, I'm not even sure if I made any sense. I was so distracted by pain, thirst and the need to go to the loo that I didn't know what I was rambling on about. Luckily, Mr Johnson appeared to be a sensible man and sorted out my problems for me. I had an ulcerated cornea. Having looked at my records, he had sense enough not to ask me if I could see the board and how many fingers he was holding up.

"You'll have to take your contact lens out," he told me, "and leave it out for a good long time. We don't know what's caused this ulcer and, by rights, you should have that eye bandaged up."

"Oh no, please don't do that," I begged him. "I haven't got another one. The left one's no good at all."

"Well . . . I'll give you some drops and some ointment to put in it. See how you go."

My contact lens tucked safely in its container and my eyes closed, I felt my way out of the hospital and home. It was impossible not to use my eye. I had to look. I had to do things at home. I just had to see. The more I did, the more agony I was in, until by late afternoon I could do nothing except pace up and down the lounge carpet in absolute torment. I have never known such pain in my life. It wasn't every few seconds the knife was being dug in now, but all the time, and being turned constantly as if my eye was being gouged out. Painkillers did nothing at all, except make my walking up and down the lounge wobbly.

By early evening, the pain was so bad I was all for chopping my head off just to get rid of it. I asked Don if he'd take me back to the hospital as I could stand it no longer. By the time we reached the hospital, I was so doped up with painkillers I kept flopping over. At least I got attention immediately. I'll remember that. The best way to get attention in a National Health hospital is to walk into reception and lie on the floor. The doctor in charge knew immediately what must be done.

"I'm sorry, you'll have to have it bandaged up. That's the only way to stop the pain and it won't heal if you keep opening and closing your eye."

Mr Johnson, bless him, had been too kind, realizing what a position he'd put me in if he'd bandaged it up earlier that day. I suppose he hoped I'd have the sense to close it. But sight is so precious to me that I'd want to see even if I had to go through agonies to do it.

There I was, back home that Wednesday evening. I had to lie down on the settee. I was so drugged I couldn't do anything else. I couldn't see. The television was blaring in the corner and Don was waiting on me with cups of tea and slices of toast. The dogs gathered round. They knew something was wrong. Bracken, with that very special sense that he alone has, kept touching me with his nose and pressing his body up against the settee to let me know that at least he was there.

For three days, I was in physical and mental agony. You would think that having been blind all those years, I would just fall naturally back into it and it wouldn't worry me. It worried me so much that I felt as if I was spending that time in hell. I couldn't see what time it was. I didn't have a Braille watch. Every time I heard Don pass, I asked him what time it was, until he got to saying, "Five minutes later than the last time you asked me" . . . not in a nasty way, but just to try and lighten the situation for me.

I tried doing all the things I would normally do. I couldn't watch television. I couldn't read the papers. I couldn't read a book. Even walking into the kitchen to make a cup of tea was like going through an obstacle course. I'd forgotten how to listen for obstacles, how to remember where doorways were. I was terrified of falling up or down steps in the garden. I lost my sense of direction completely and had to go back to feeling walls and fences to find my way into the house. The mental torment of blindness was overpowering. It made me physically sick. It turned me off my food. The thought of spending the rest of my life in that dark hell was totally unbearable.

Most of those three days were spent sitting on the settee, grieving for sight. My life had changed so much since that successful operation almost ten years ago. I was geared to a visual life. I might have my problems — how small they seemed! Playing Russian roulette with the traffic outside, that was nothing, not compared to blindness. There would be no more dog shows. I couldn't take the dogs for a walk any more and appreciate the woods and the park. I wouldn't be able to walk up those paths and look at the changing scene, pick brilliant red leaves up and rootle about in the grass underneath the trees for the toadstools that sprang up in their different colours and different shapes. And how many sunsets would I miss? How many rainbows? I had never missed one in the last ten years. At the slightest hint of a rainbow, I am standing out in our back garden getting sopping wet. There would be no more television-watching or magazine-reading. I wouldn't be able to go down to the local library and peruse the shelves.

The thoughts that crowded in on me were horrific. Although I was advised to keep the bandages on for a week, after three days panic set in and I tore them off. The relief as the light and colours crowded in on me was incredible. It was still painful to look, but I cut some of that out by wearing dark glasses and promised myself that I would spend most of the time with my eyes closed. But I had to know that, at any time, I could open that eye and see. I still found it difficult to get about: the clarity of vision had gone and, although the colours and brilliance were still there, everything was hazy, blurred.

The following week I was back in the chaotic National Health system, waiting my turn to see Mr Johnson. I sat there with everything crossed. I was going to ask him about the left eye. After all, Mr Shearing had never given up on it. He had told me that he would try again. It was far more difficult than the right eye had been but there was hope, and now I realized how much I needed "a spare". The sight through my left eye was non-existent, although I was convinced I could see when a light was switched on or off and I thought I could see the shape of a window in a room. So where there was some vision, I told myself, there was hope.

Mr Johnson reassured me that the right cornea was healing, probably slower than normal because I wouldn't keep it bandaged up, but at least he understood my panic at being condemned to total darkness, even for a few days.

"I don't think I would put the contact lens back in."

"What about glasses?" I asked him. "I have an old pair at home."

"Oh yes, you can wear your glasses. I want you to come and see me in another three weeks and we'll reappraise the contact lens situation."

"I'm sure it can't be the lens," I told him. I loved my contact lens. It was so comfortable normally. I could see much better through a contact lens than glasses. I hated wearing glasses.

"We'll see," he said.

I could feel the queue leaning up against the door and the need for patients to pass through quickly but I was determined not to go until I'd asked my very important question.

"What about my left eye? Mr Shearing did say that he would try again in the future. I really feel I need it now, especially after this."

As he switched the little light on to look in my eye, I sat, hardly daring to breath, hoping and praying.

"Hmm, well . . . I don't know about this," he muttered under his breath. "Can you see anything through it?"

"I think so. I think I can see light and dark."

I covered up the right eye while he switched his examination light on and off. I heard the soft clicks of the light switch.

"I can see it now," I said.

"Can you follow the light?"

I tried moving the left eye here and there.

"Is it on now?"

"No," I said.

He moved back on his stool and looked at me. "I don't think you can see anything out of there."

"But I can," I told him. "I can see the frame of a window. I can see when the light's on and off."

He shook his head and took another instrument from his desk. "I'll just check the eye pressure." He examined my left eye with the pressure-reading instrument and then sat back, rubbing his chin. "The pressure is sixty-three," he said, seriously.

"What does that mean?"

"It means that there is no vision in the left eye. There can't be, not under that sort of pressure."

"But how can I see light and dark? There must be vision!"

"The optic nerve is dead," he told me. "It can't survive under that type of pressure."

"But . . ." I was going to try and convince him I could see through it.

"It's your imagination," he said. "It's because you want to see through it. It could be the brain accepting some sort of light in, but it certainly isn't the eye. I'm afraid there is nothing I, nor anyone else, can do until they can replace eyes and optic nerves completely."

Fear and self-pity gripped me. I wanted that left eye. I'd always felt it was there as a spare. What if my cornea had been damaged completely? I wouldn't have been able to see ever again. I couldn't face that life, not blindness. I couldn't take it now. I'd had sight, which to me was the elixir of life. I tried to say "thank you", but the lump in my throat got in the way and I made a hasty retreat from his consulting room. I couldn't face the friend who had kindly taken me to the hospital. I made a beeline for the ladies and sat and sobbed. That didn't help at all, it only gave me a headache and a very sore right eye. I told myself I was damn lucky to see at all.

Back home, I tried to make light of the situation to Don and just told him that the left eye had shot its bolt and that was the end of that. That afternoon, I rummaged round in the drawers to find my old pair of glasses. They were there all right, a bit scratched but I could look round the scratches. It was wonderful when I put them on, to have clarity and outlines to everything I could see but, oh, the distortion! I'd forgotten how big they made everything and my brain just couldn't cope with the different sizes. All the dogs looked like donkeys and six-inch steps turned into six-feet heights. I fell downstairs three times. Even though the glasses were made of a plastic type of material, they still drove my nose insane and caused soreness behind the ears. I just don't know how anyone can wear glasses. They are antiquated. They steam up. They get dirty and they distort everything.

I was longing to wear my contact lens again and when it came back from being checked at the lens centre, with a note saying everything was well, I put it back in. Immediately, I felt that too-familiar stinging sensation. I removed it. It was only then I noticed the bottle of cleaning fluid I had bought just before going on holiday. It was unlike my normal bottle. I donned my glasses, picked it up and examined the writing: "Hard or gas permeable contact lens only." I read the small print on the back: "Not to be used with soft contact lens." I was horrified. Was this liquid responsible for all that agony? I rang the contact lens centre immediately. Yes, that liquid would cause all my eye problems. A soft contact lens soaks up the solution in which it is being cleaned. Once in the eye, the lens releases the solution.

I know I had definitely asked the chemist for soft contact lens cleaning fluid. I had been given the wrong one by mistake, and what a mistake. I hope it never happens to anyone else. I wouldn't wish that agony on my worst enemy, not even the VAT man!

CHAPTER TWELVE

THE VAT MAN COMETH

A few years ago, I was advised to start a limited company. I was told that it would be easier for tax purposes, as my money came in irregular lumps. It was the worst piece of advice I ever took. I am totally useless with money and figures, and I ended up in an awful mess. I innocently believed that the money that came into the company was mine — I was the only one earning it — but I was wrong.

I was horrified when I realized that I had to pay VAT and put in regular returns. The money came in lump sums and couldn't be spread over a year, or years, and on occasions it put me into the VAT-paying bracket. I didn't do the VAT returns. I had someone working for me and felt that she was doing a good job. It wasn't until we closed the company that I realized no-one had put in VAT returns. We had been paying on assessment only.

It would be easy to lay the blame at someone else's door but, as a director of the company, it was my responsibility. The crunch came when someone from the VAT offices visited me to check the books. She was a nice little lady and I felt quite sorry for her. It must be awful being a VAT person, I thought, so I was determined to be very pleasant and co-operative. After all, I thought, my VAT returns have all been done. Everything is in perfect order. Maybe if I had known the truth I would have been a little less friendly, for when the letter came from the VAT office a fortnight later, it stated, in big, black lettering, that I owed them *one thousand, five hundred pounds*! I passed the letter silently over to Don, pushing it in front of his porridge bowl. He dropped his spoon in shock.

"You can't owe them any money. I thought all the VAT returns had been done."

"So did I. They must have made a mistake," I said. "I'll give them a ring this morning."

"No mistake," I was told by a very unfriendly voice. "Your VAT returns have been paid on assessment for the last four years and this outstanding amount must be paid immediately."

I realized, with horror, that I better learn how to do VAT returns . . . and quickly.

"Fifteen per cent of that, and divide by this . . ." the accountant rattled on over the phone, as I begged him to tell me how to produce a VAT figure. I wrote it all down and tried to make sense of it. I have never been any good at maths. At least I have an excuse: I could never see the blackboard when the teachers were showing us how to work the sums out and, not having a mathematical brain, I have never really wanted to catch up on my maths education. I was thrown in at the deep end. There I was, with my little calculator and piles of books strewn all over the dining room table, trying to do four years' of VAT returns in seven days. Sadly, I came to roughly the same conclusion as the VAT man. I hadn't a clue what to do about it. I didn't have fifteen hundred pounds to give the VAT man.

Whenever I'm in total despair — quite frequently these days it seems — I take the dogs out for a walk. It somehow brings a perspective to life . . . a reality. It gives me back all the right values. I put Bracken, Katy and Teak on their leads and decided I'd walk up Baulk Lane to the fields, where the view over Nottingham is stunning. I often wonder if the dogs think I'm going crackers. When I set out down the drive to play my Russian roulette with the road outside, I know I'm very twitched-up and agitated. And that particular day, when I was trying to work out my VAT problems, I was distraught, almost physically sick with worry, as I stood waiting for the traffic to cease, the three dogs sitting patiently by me at the kerb. Teak was hopping about a little on her front feet and giving the occasional whine. Katy looked up at me with a really serious expression on her face. Whenever she's worried, the black fur between her eyes stands up and gives her a wild look. Bracken pushed his cold nose into my hand and I looked down at them. I do hope there was no-one passing at that point, because I decided I should reassure the dogs that my bad humour wasn't aimed at them.

"I'm sorry, you lot. I'm not angry with you. It's that rotten VAT man!"

As I climbed up Baulk Lane and over the motorway bridge into the field, so my spirits rose. The three dogs knew I needed cheering up. Katy went off instantly, nose to the ground, tail waving, snuffling amongst the long grass. I knew she was looking for something to bring me. Instinctively, I held my hand out on her return. Her tail wagged furiously as she bounced up and down with eagerness to please.

"Clever girl!" I praised, as I took her prize off her. I didn't need to look at what I was holding . . . I could smell it. It was a large, dried-out cowpat. Dogs really have a wonderful way of bringing you down to earth. I laughed hysterically as the thought of what I would really like to do with that cowpat came into my mind. The dogs shared the humour and danced about, barking with glee.

I stood there, my hands held well away from my body (I wasn't quite sure what to do with them) and I realized that whatever happened to me, no-one could take this pleasure away. The VAT man couldn't claim the bit of sight I had. He couldn't take my joy of seeing and being with the dogs away from me. I can recommend a dog walk to anyone who is feeling miserable. Nothing worries me when I'm out in the fields. No phones can ring. No little letter-box can clatter with a brown envelope and no-one can knock at the door, because I'm not there.

Refreshed and confident on my return home, I wrote to the VAT man. I explained that although I was responsible for sending in the VAT returns, I was convinced that it had been done correctly by someone else. I explained that I didn't have the finances to pay the fifteen hundred pounds immediately, but I would do my utmost to clear the debt as soon as possible. I was sure that these people were human beings. They would understand mistakes and give me time. I posted that letter on the 18 January 1985. No letter of acknowledgement or acceptance was returned to me. Well, being a person who feels you should let sleeping dogs lie, I didn't attempt to contact them, apart from putting in my up-to-date VAT returns and paying as much as I could afford monthly.

In the meantime, I thought I should try to get a job. Although I haven't any specific training to offer, only my experience as a telephonist, I felt sure that my enthusiasm and need to earn money would see me through. Oh yes, there was a job shortage and queues at the dole office, but were they really trying? Did they want work? I knew I did. And so, without really knowing what I was going to do, my job search began. I scoured the evening papers.

The first vacancy I saw that I fancied was a type of sales job, something I'd never thought of in the past, but very unusual . . . selling cable television. That appealed. I'm the original square-eyes when it comes to watching television.

It wasn't a one-off type of interview but a meeting at one of Nottingham's hotels, where those who were interested were invited along to listen to the job description and view some of the television channels that were on offer. Dressed in my most respectable suit and wearing make-up, I hotfooted it across the city to my first job interview with great enthusiasm and complete faith in the fact that I would be offered a job.

My first shock was to find that the interview room was full of men . . . not a female in sight. All, I was to learn later, the hard-bitten salesmen type from the double-glazing and home-improvement firms. I hid myself away in a dark corner to listen to the job description. It wasn't cold-calling. Only homes that were already linked up to cable would be visited. Having been supplied with the full information, we were then treated to about an hour of tele-watching. That cheered me up. I was even keener. They were offering a great deal, I had to admit it. Towards the end of the meeting, I began to think how I would cope. I didn't have a car, but there were plenty of buses around. I could easily catch buses to the area allotted to me for the day. How would I go on in the dark evenings when I couldn't see? I'd feel my way from gate to gate, I told myself.

All the problems that nagged at the back of my mind were pushed away by my total enthusiasm. Where there's a will there's a way, I constantly repeated mentally. I filled in the appropriate forms and left, still convinced that I would soon be a sales representative. A few days later, I received a telephone call from the company. At least they had the grace to ring me and thank me for my application, but . . . and what a "but"! I had no idea how depressing it was to be unwanted. How inadequate and useless I felt! Why had they turned me down? Because I was a woman? Because I couldn't see enough to drive a car? Or both? Whatever the reasons, my ego was totally flattened.

Over the next few months, I applied for various jobs — as a telephonist, doing telephone sales, etc. — and was turned down for all of them. I can now understand and have great sympathy for anyone who has been out of a job for a long period. It takes an enormous amount of courage, and guts, and willpower to keep looking, only to be rejected. I felt mentally and physically bruised. I wanted to creep into a corner and lick my wounds.

Still, we were managing and Don was doing his very best. I hope he'll forgive me, though, when I tell you that he works long and hard but he won't charge enough for his services. I once did a survey round the local chiropodists. They were all charging nearly double. I can't convince Don that he's worth a lot more as a chiropodist than anyone else I know, but then I'm biased and I won't change him now. He has that sort of temperament and that's why I love him.

Looking on the brighter side, I hadn't heard anything from the VAT man and it was now September. As luck would have it, on 25 September I had to give a talk in York to help raise money for the Guide Dogs for the Blind Association. I had managed to get a friend to take me in our car. I spent a lovely day there with dog-loving people and experiencing Yorkshire hospitality, and didn't get home until late that night, so Don and I didn't have much chance to talk. The next day he told me the bad news. A man had come from the VAT office to take the car away. It was registered in the company name and they wanted to seize it to pay off the money I owed them, which had now gone down to nine hundred pounds. I couldn't believe it.

"Did you explain to them about my letter and my payments?" I asked Don.

"Yes, of course I did, but he didn't want to listen. You had better ring them this morning."

I rang them. I don't know why. I'd have been better employed beating my head against a brick wall. The cold, unfriendly voice on the other end of the line told me I had fourteen days to pay. I asked him why there had been no reply to the letter I sent in January and why there had been no warning. His attitude seemed to be that they didn't need to warn people, or answer letters. Over lunch, I told Don their reply. I find it very comforting to share my problems with him. He can be guaranteed to come up with a solution.

"Well, go and see the bank manager for a start and write them another letter."

The problem is they are used to dealing with people who try to avoid paying VAT and who are probably living in comparative luxury. We certainly weren't. I managed to buy the dogs' food from money I'd earned from pet dog training classes. It just about covered it weekly and I'd been through the house with a fine tooth comb, cutting down on every conceivable thing, so that I could save just a little every week to pay off the VAT man. Instead of four teabags going into the teapot, it had been cut down to three. I had decided not to eat lunch, for two reasons: number one, it was cheaper, and number two, it helped me lose weight. Milk was another thing. We seemed to use such a lot of it. I blamed Don and Kerensa for pouring it all over their breakfast cereals. When I stopped taking milk in my tea, I realized who the true culprit was. We saved seven pints of milk a week when I took tea without it. The heating bills for our home seemed phenomenal. Of course, Don was heating his surgery, but in the daytime, when no-one used the house except me, it was far too expensive to have heating on just to keep me warm when I could put a jacket on instead. I did and slashed nearly a hundred pounds off our winter heating bill.

I wrote almost a novel to the VAT man, explaining my circumstances and said that I was obviously willing to pay. If he would check on his records, he would see I had already paid six hundred pounds. And I went to see the bank manager, in fear and trepidation. He was my last resort and my bank account wasn't in a very healthy state. He was quite surprised at my treatment from the VAT office.

"Normally," he said, "with companies, they are quite

happy if some money is paid off and willingness is there. Try paying them three hundred pounds," he told me.

The three hundred was like rubbing salt into open wounds. It infuriated the VAT office so much that they sent a man round. I have always been aware that Bracken has no finesse regarding human characters. When I opened the door to the VAT man, Bracken rushed from the lounge to greet him. To put it mildly, I could have throttled him.

The VAT man stood on the doorstep reading me the riot act. I certainly wasn't going to ask him in. Bracken fussed about him as if he was a dog food representative, and then took the opportunity to "water" the bush Don had just planted at the side of our front door. My Bracken was lured to the beautiful little evergreen. Every opportunity, he shot out of the front door to cock his leg on it. It infuriated Don and it didn't do the bush any good either. I'm sure Bracken aimed at it this time, but he was so excited by our visitor that he missed the bush altogether, but managed to catch the VAT man's left leg nicely. I knew I shouldn't have laughed, but I just couldn't help it. I was in hysterics. His face was a positive picture of disgust.

Don and I laughed about it for months, and when I went to tell the bank manager that the VAT people were insisting on the full payment and what Bracken had done to the caller, he agreed immediately that I could borrow the rest of the outstanding sum.

He's the sort of bank manager I'd like to keep in my wardrobe.

CHAPTER THIRTEEN

OUR RUSSIAN EXPERIENCE

Most people have ups and downs in their lives but mine's like a roller coaster. One moment I'm hurling to the depths of despair, the next I'm on a high, living like a celebrity. When I drag myself out of bed in the morning, I never know what sort of day it's going to be. It certainly makes for variety of life, but it doesn't do my nerves any good.

The first day of August was going to be rather peculiar. There was a phone call in the morning and a man's deep voice, with a very thick foreign accent, asked for Sheila Ho-Can.

"Yes, speaking," I said cautiously.

"Is this you?"

"Yes, this is me speaking."

He then began to ramble on so quickly I could hardly understand a word he said. I caught things like "ov" and "meeting you" . . . "writer" . . . "ship in Tilbury Docks", and "Intourist Mos-cow".

I stood with the phone pressed to my ear in total astonishment. Moscow! The Russians were after me now! No, it was Stan down the road . . . he was playing a prank. He was really good at doing Russian accents. I began to giggle.

"Hello. . . ?" the voice resounded in my ear. "Are you still there, Mrs Ho-Can?"

"Yes . . . yes, I'm still here." I thought I'd play him along, just to see what the joke turned out to be.

"Will you come on the twelfth?"

"Will I come where?"

"Tilbury Docks. Mr Kulov will be waiting for you on the Klavdia Elanskaya liner."

At that point I was tempted to say, "Oh, come on Stan, stop messing about." Luckily, I didn't. "August the twelfth? No I don't think I'm doing anything on August the twelfth," I told him politely. "I'm sure I could be at Tilbury Docks."

"Very good, Mrs Ho-Can. Mr Kulov will be delighted to see you. Would you like to take my number here at Intourist Mos-cow?"

He gave me a London number and, for the first time, I began to think that this was for real.

"You will receive confirmation in writing. Good day, Mrs Ho-Can."

I stood for quite a time with the phone still in my hand, listening to the dialling tone. If it was Stan, this London number certainly wasn't Intourist Moscow. I dialled it. After only two rings, a female voice announced this was Intourist Moscow. I replaced the receiver as Don came in from the surgery for his morning coffee.

"Petal, I've just had the strangest call. They said they were from Intourist Moscow and it was something about us going down to Tilbury to meet a Russian man on a boat."

Don looked pointedly across at the calendar. "Oh, it's August," he said.

"Yes, they want me to go down on August the twelfth."

"I thought it might be April Fools' Day." He grinned at me. "That'll be Stan. You know what he's like."

"No, it wasn't Stan. Look, here's the number." I passed him the piece of paper. "I've just rung them back. It really was Intourist Moscow."

"Wait a minute . . . wait a minute. Now, tell me again, who are we meeting . . . where?"

"I don't really know," I confessed. "I just managed to get a bit about a man from Russia coming to England and for you and I to go and meet him."

"Ha, knowing Stan he'd have found the number of Intourist Moscow to make it look good."

"Oh well, I'll just have to wait for the letter of confirmation to come," I said. "I don't know what it's all about."

The letter came the very next day, with bold red headings stating "Intourist Moscow".

"There you are," I said to Don, as I pushed it towards his cereal bowl. "Look at that."

We both read the letter twice over in disbelief.

Mr Sharshinby Kulov is delighted that you have
accepted his invitation to have dinner and spend
the evening with him on the Klavdia Elanskaya
at Tilbury Docks on 12 August.

The letter went on to explain that Mr Kulov was a Soviet writer who had heard about my book, *Emma and I*, and wanted to meet us.

The next few days, Don and I talked of nothing else. We had never met anyone from the USSR and although I knew Don was just as keen and excited as I was at our forthcoming trip, he started making little jokes. "Once they get us on that ship, they won't let us off," he said. "Maybe they want to enrol you as a spy!"

"A spy with one eye," I laughed.

I desperately wanted to take one of the dogs — preferably Bracken — to meet our Russian friends, but telephone enquiries to the vet warned me off. A Russian ship would be Russian soil and maybe Bracken would be clamped in quarantine after stepping off the ship. I daren't take that risk. Instead, I filled my bag with photographs of the dogs.

It was a glorious summer afternoon as Don and I travelled "dogless" to Tilbury. I wondered if they liked dogs in Russia. Did they have them as pets? Did they have dog shows and were there tins of dog food in the shops? I wondered all sorts of stupid things. Their culture seems so different from ours, from the glimpses we receive on the media, and it was hard for me to imagine meeting Russian people.

We arrived at Tilbury and found the passenger liner. We stood, about to mount the gangway, when Don took hold of my hand and stopped me.

"This could be it, petal. This could be goodbye England."

"Don't be silly," I said. "What could they want us for over there?"

A pretty young girl with long, blonde, flowing hair ran to greet us. "You are Sheila and Don?" she said, in almost perfect English.

"Yes," we said.

"I am your interpreter. Please come this way. Mr Kulov is longing to meet you."

"She's pretty," Don whispered in my ear. "I thought all these women were big, fat, strong and ugly."

The moment we stepped into the reception area of the liner, we were approached by yet more pretty young girls, two of them with their long blonde hair worn in two plaits. They carried between them a huge platter. On the platter sat the biggest loaf of bread I have ever seen in my life. Both Don and I stood there, not knowing quite what to say or do. The girls gave us brilliant smiles and moved the giant loaf a little closer. Don's eyebrows suddenly shot up and he put his hands out from his sides in a puzzled gesture.

"We can't take that, petal," he said, out of the corner of his mouth. "It's too big. We'd never get it in the boot."

I'm not sure whether our interpreter heard but she came to the rescue. "This is friendship bread. You take a piece and sprinkle salt on it. It's very nice."

A look of relief spread over Don's face, as we took our piece of friendship bread.

Mr Kulov was a short man with dark hair and glasses, and a warm and friendly face. He stretched his arms out to greet me, kissed me as if I were a long lost daughter, and shook Don warmly by the hand. The awful thing was that he couldn't speak English and we, of course, couldn't speak his language. The pretty girl stood a little to one side interpreting, while our host told us where he lived.

"Oh, is that in Russia?" I looked at him and then at our interpreter. She didn't bother to repeat my words.

"Not Russia," she corrected, "the Soviet Union."

"Ah. Well is Mr Kulov Russian?" I asked.

"No . . . no, he's a Soviet citizen." She said it with fervour. I was soon to learn that I must refer to everyone as Soviet citizens.

Mr Kulov took us on an inspection tour of the liner. I'd never been on a big ship before and to see the bridge was fascinating. Every single person we met seemed overjoyed and greeted us as bosom friends, except the two men that followed us everywhere like huge menacing shadows (that's how Don put it anyway). They looked like twins — tall, about six foot broad, with blond hair and piercing blue eyes. Don was convinced they were KGB men.

"Look at that one," he said, "the one on the left. He's got a bulge just below the armpit. Shall we make a run for it now?"

I'm sure I don't know what Mr Kulov thought. I hope the impression I gave was of giggling with delight and not at the suggestions Don was whispering in my ear.

Over dinner, I asked Mr Kulov (through the interpreter, of course) how he'd heard of me. Apparently, there had been reports in the Soviet papers of my miraculous operation and of how wonderful Emma had been.

"Do you have a dog?" I asked him.

He immediately fetched out his wallet and produced a picture of a German shepherd. "A very much loved pet," he assured me. We exchanged stories of our families and homes and I asked if Mr Kulov couldn't come and visit us and our home. He'd be very welcome to stay with us, I added. Our invitation was politely sidestepped by a counter-invitation that we must come to the Soviet Union and stay with him.

I had the strangest feeling, while eating my dinner and exchanging pleasantries with our Soviet friends. I felt I was back in the 'fifties, a young child in the company of adults. I realized it was the feeling of respect these people showed towards one another. I noticed that the waiters were speaking to the elders of each table first. They had an air of being polite and helpful, without being subservient, as if their task of waiting on table was a pleasure. Throughout the evening, both Don and I noticed how all the younger members of the crew approached their elders with deep respect.

At the end of the meal, vodka glasses were placed out on the table. Don smiled.

"Vodka?" he said to Sharshinby.

Mr Kulov nodded. "Vodka!" Obviously a universal word. The glasses were filled to the brim with the innocent looking alcohol. Sharshinby raised his glass. "*Nastarovie!*"

As Don and I watched intently, he downed it in one. Don raised his glass, repeating the Russian word, "*Nastarovie*", and, not wishing to look cowardly where alcohol was concerned, he, too, downed it in one. I watched in amazement, as Don's face turned from its normal pale pink to deep purple. I knew he wanted to gasp for air but — a gentleman to the last — he made a smile (more of a grimace) and his eyes watered. I was no fool. I took a gentle sip, but still the fiery liquid blazoned its way down my throat.

No sooner had Don replaced his empty glass on the table than it was filled to the brim by an eager waiter. Don's expression was a picture. Warmth and eagerness filled his face, caused obviously by the first glass of vodka. But there was a tinge of something else in his eyes. He looked like a little boy who was being made to take a second spoonful of medicine.

Over the vodka, I learnt that Sharshinby had been a casualty of the Second World War, receiving injuries that had caused poor eyesight. Therefore he'd read with great interest and concern the article about me in the Soviet newspapers. So moved was he by my story of blindness and my guide dog Emma, that he wrote a poem especially for me. This poem had been widely published in the Soviet Union and now was included in a book of poetry.

Poor Don had had to reverse one of his cardinal rules, which was "always empty a glass immediately it is placed in front of you." He sat cradling the glass in his hand and whispered to me, "This isn't like English vodka, you know. It must be 106 degree proof. It's a good job I arranged for somebody to drive us home. Another glass of this and I shan't remember where we live."

We were then told that they had invited some guests from a Soviet friendship group in England and there was entertainment laid on for us. I felt like a queen. As we were led through the dining rooms and leisure areas to the ballroom, where the evening's entertainment was to take place, Don pointed out that on almost every table were chessboards. I know he would have loved to have spent the evening playing chess. Pitting his wits against the Soviet Masters was one of his dreams, but we were in for a much more exciting evening.

As we were led into the ballroom, it was announced to

the hundred or so visitors and crew that we were the special guests of the evening. We were treated to dance, music and singing Soviet-style and then came the speeches, all translated into English for our benefit. Mr Kulov told his own story about me — a little slanted, but related with great feeling. I was a child, in his eyes, who the State had ignored. My mother fought to keep us alive, working twenty-six hours a day for the money to pay for an operation for me. After years of toil and deprivation, she managed to afford the exorbitant fee asked by our Health Service.

When it was my turn to give the speech, I tried, kindly but firmly, to put the record straight and insisted that our Health Service was free and it was only lack of medical technology that had stopped me seeing, not lack of money.

After the speeches came the presentations . . . to me! I was overwhelmed by the generosity. Mr Kulov had a friendship hat especially for me and then presents for all of us, not only Don and myself but my mum and dad and the dogs. There were bars of dog chocolates for them and dog biscuits. For me, along with the beautiful friendship hat, came material to make a dress, jewellery boxes, a set of vodka glasses, and for my mum and dad, a beautiful tea set, boxes of cigarettes and chocolates, books about the Soviet Union and, a treasured little gift, Mr Kulov's own book of poetry.

At last it was time to go and I had the chance to say my one and only word of Russian — *Dosvidania* . . . Goodbye.

"Well, petal," Don said, "we got away."

"Oh, don't be mean. They were so nice."

"Yes, they were. They were lovely people," he agreed.

We had been treated like royalty for an evening. It was lovely. I have kept in touch with Mr Kulov, a little spasmodically. I think, perhaps, there are times when my letters don't get through to him. I received a beautiful copper picture of Emma a few months after our visit which has pride of place in my kitchen.

Emma certainly introduced me to many people and made me many friends. Even now, six years after her death, the friendships are still coming in her name.

CHAPTER FOURTEEN

PSYCHE

The next morning, 13 August, I received a letter from the bank. They were suggesting I paid some of the money back I had borrowed the previous year. Back to the "Sits. Vac." column with a vengeance! I did manage to find a job of sorts, but definitely the wrong type for anyone in my situation. It was working for a loan company on a self-employed basis. I was responsible for placing ads in local papers, filling out forms over the telephone for applicants wishing to borrow money and sending them off to the head office. Not one of them was accepted. I ended up with a large advertising bill . . . and even more depressed. Out of the people that rang me, ninety-nine per cent of them were desperate. Many were miners still suffering from the effects of the strike and in peril of having their homes repossessed. The experience should have made me grateful for my small mercies, but it didn't. It just depressed me all the more.

The dogs provided me with an outlet . . . a release. I felt, at a dog show, I could be free of all my worries. But even that didn't work. Katy had done very well as a youngster, winning her first novice class at eleven months — quite young, especially for a Labrador. But, along with everything else, even this side of my life seemed to go wrong and it was all my fault. Whenever I walked into the ring at a dog show with Katy, I went to pieces. I became nervous, uptight, and a little voice inside my head told me, You're no good at training dogs. What are you doing at a dog show? You're no good at anything. Go home and sit in a corner!

Poor Katy felt all these emotions and, consequently, her work suffered. She became so miserable the moment we stepped into the ring that we never got placed. She began to break her stays — something she'd never done in the past two years. I was all for giving up dog shows and I had an excuse. Katy came into season and I decided to find her a mate.

It's a sad fact that many breeds of dog suffer from hereditary defects and I have always done my best to ensure that the breeding stock I use is first class. One of the hereditary defects that Labradors suffer from is hip dysplasia. The hip joints don't fit into the sockets correctly or are misshapen, and often this causes arthritis.

Before I bred from any of the Labradors, I had them X-rayed. Katy's hips were fine and I had been given the okay by my vet to mate her. But now to find a "husband". I wanted something very special for Katy because I intended to keep one of the puppies. He had to be black, intelligent and clever, and free from any hereditary defects. I combed the nation and found a suitable dog in Wales. Wales was an awful long way to go to take Katy, and there was a costly stud fee and petrol expenses . . . but Don and I managed to scrape the money from somewhere. I'm so thankful we did.

I have a firm belief that has kept me going through life, that whatever happens, however bad things are, it's all for some purpose. But I didn't realize that taking Katy to mate Gunstock Teal in Wales would someday change my whole way of life and thinking.

Sixty-five days after our visit to Wales, Katy produced her litter — nine puppies, all black. Seven bitches and two dogs.

I was delighted. I wanted to keep a bitch and now I'd have a really good choice. As this litter was so important to me, I spent every possible moment with the puppies, watching their development and growth. I made notes of which puppy opened its eyes first, and which one got up on four legs and tottered around the box, who was the first to bark . . . I knew I was going to have a terrible job choosing which one was to stay, so I made up my mind that the temperament tests would be the all-important thing.

I knew exactly what type of temperament I needed. I wanted a bitch, and a dominant one. One that was full of life and interested in what was going on around her. I was so excited the day of the temperament tests. I felt like a six-year-old opening a Christmas stocking. There was one little bitch who was long and lithe and had such a length of tail it reminded me of one of those long liquorice sticks I used to chew on as a child. Her nose was pointed, her ears were an odd shape, but she was definitely the one. She was full of life and eagerness, alert to every sound and sight, a bundle of sheer joy and mischief. I chose a very apt name for her . . . Psyche. The dictionary definition means "breath of life".

The first few weeks of Psyche's reign — for that's undoubtedly what she did over the household — was almost too much for me. I began to think I was getting too old to have a puppy around. One minute she was chewing the table leg, the next she was hurling herself upstairs to get up to some mischief in my bedroom. Kerensa was then eight, just the right age to cement a relationship with a puppy and, as Psyche was so active, she was given the job of playing with her. They played hour after hour, neither of them tiring.

As Psyche grew and developed, I began to think that Katy had sneaked out one night, for Psyche didn't look much like a Labrador. She was long and slender. Her pointed nose had grown even further, and her ears . . . they had grown outwards. They looked like tulip leaves stuck on the side of her head. Luckily, I've never been one to take looks into account. Temperament is the most important asset to me and Psyche's temperament reminds me of a giggly schoolgirl. Whenever she wags her tail, everything, right up to the end of her nose, wags and wriggles.

She turned out to be a lunatic on legs. She would never greet me delicately, like her mum, Katy, but hurl herself from a great distance at me. Around the garden, she was just as batty. One of our gates is wrought iron. Psyche would hurl herself at it, thrusting her head through the bars and get stuck. Day after day I would release her in the hope that she'd learnt her lesson. She could get her head in the gate, but not get it back out again. It was a great challenge to me to harness Psyche's power source without damping down her zest for life.

Living with Psyche was just like having constant sunshine. She was such a pleasure to be with, but I had to adjust. Psyche was very quick, both mentally and physically, and I had become accustomed to slow, plodding, Labradors. Or maybe it was me. Perhaps I was slowing down with old age. But, whatever it was, Psyche was much too quick for me. I always spend the first few months of a puppy's life socializing it to traffic, people, shops, and strange noises. Psyche hated heavy traffic, so it meant frequent trips into Stapleford, our local shopping area.

Saturday morning was Psyche's socializing hour, when the cars and buses revved, bumper to bumper, along the main Derby Road. Kerensa normally accompanied us, because she took a great interest in Psyche's training. But something had lured her to the television, so Psyche and I went alone. We had just passed a crowd of mums and toddlers on foot and in pushchairs when one of the little darlings let out an almighty scream, followed by wails of "Bo-Bo gone!" As I travelled nonchalantly on my way, I heard the fading screams and mum's arguments of, "Well, you had him a minute ago . . . what have you done with him?"

It wasn't until Psyche and I reached the cake shop that all became clear. I was just telling her to "sit and stay" while I popped into the shop when I noticed that her normally slender black muzzle seemed enlarged and bulging. She emitted soft whining noises that meant, I've got something really nice in my mouth. Would you like to share it with me? She opened her jaws and let half an orange teddy bear drop into my hands. She had devoured an arm, a leg and an ear and was obviously looking forward to finishing off the remainder.

There was no way I could return it to that poor little child and, in all honesty, I'm a coward. I should have gone back and owned up, but instead I stuffed the poor little teddy in the bottom of my bag.

Training a dog for competition is very different from training an average pet. There is far more precision required. Not only does the dog have to sit, she has to do it quickly and in the right place. I suppose it would be easy to browbeat a dog into precision work but that's not the way I train. I want my dogs to enjoy their work and to approach their competitions with enthusiasm. Each exercise must be geared around play, taught as a game. At six months of age, Psyche refused to play with me. The instant I produced a squeaky toy or a knotted pair of tights from out of my pocket, she froze and turned into granite. It was as if she was gritting her teeth and sinking her paws into the ground. Her ears went back and stuck out like half-wilted tulip leaves. She wouldn't budge an inch.

For a while, I began to panic. Had I chosen the wrong puppy, or was it me? Of course it was me. Katy had been so easy to train, so quick to learn, that I expected Psyche to be the same. Although Katy was Psyche's mum, their temperaments were entirely different. I had to re-think my whole training methods.

Despite the fact that Psyche appeared to be very dominant, she also lacked confidence. A new exercise and she was afraid to do it. I needed to approach her training carefully and slowly, showing her each little exercise over and over again. I realized that toys weren't her main interest in life. She wanted to play with me. Her idea of playing with me was leaping all over me and her teeth were a big part of the game. She would leap up in an effort to bite the end of my nose, or chase after me and grab my arm. We would play together like a pair of mad dogs in the park. More often than not, my anorak and jumpers would be ripped and holey and my arms would be scarred with teeth-marks. She would never actually bite aggressively, but to bite is a dog's natural way of playing and as long as we both enjoyed ourselves, that's all that mattered.

I did find one item that Psyche loved playing with and that was a sock of Don's. Don is typical of most men, as far as socks are concerned. He often forgets to put clean ones on and, when he does, the dirty ones lie at the side of the bed. Psyche's nose told her every time Don changed his socks, for she would sneak upstairs and grab one. Not keen on the smell of sweaty socks, I managed to wean her onto his clean ones. I'd rummage through his drawers — when he wasn't looking, of course — and find a sock I felt sure was an odd one. Psyche would do anything for a sock. We'd go in the park and train and then play, throwing or hiding Don's socks. The problem was they didn't last very long. They either got ripped up or too soggy, so I was getting through about five odd socks a week.

"Petal!" Don called down the stairs one morning. "I can't find any socks that match. Are they all in the wash?"

"They must be," I lied. "Or they could have got pushed under the bed. I'll have a look for you later." I made a mental note to go out and buy him some new socks and swore Psyche to secrecy.

Psyche at eight weeks, dominating our remaining plants

Bracken snoozing on the settee, as usual

Bracken

Buttons

Psyche at one year old, showing her long nose

Kerensa with Pip Squeak at six weeks

Katy looking very proud of her new litter.
Kerensa is holding Psyche

Don and I with Bracken, Katy and Psyche

Three weeks later, the game was up. Don returned from a walk one morning, came into the kitchen and laid a soggy sock on the draining board.

"Psyche found that on the park," he told me. "It was just near the cricket pitch. Isn't it funny?—it's exactly the same as your mother bought me last Christmas."

I don't know whether he suspected anything, but I had to own up. I now buy him and Psyche socks by the dozen.

I had great hopes for Psyche as far as competition obedience was concerned and I felt now, at long last, I was breeding Labradors with a super temperament and working ability. I was even beginning to plan Psyche's first litter but before that could be considered, she had to be X-rayed for hip dysplasia. At a year old, I booked her in at the vet's for her X-rays. She was so agile and athletic, I was convinced her hips were perfect. When I returned to collect her in the afternoon, the vet greeted me with a grim face.

"Come and have a look at the X-rays." He showed me into the surgery and placed the X-rays on the lighted screen.

Psyche's hips were terrible. The heads were badly shaped and ill-fitting. I was appalled. That was the end of my breeding line, the finish of all my hopes for the future. I vowed, there and then in the vet's surgery, I would never breed again. Psyche would be spayed after her first season. I returned home with a very heavy heart and within ten minutes of getting back from the surgery I received two phone calls. The first one was from the Labrador Rescue Service in Nottingham to say that they had re-homed one of my chocolate Labradors. He was four years old. As a puppy, he'd gone to a family I was convinced would make perfect owners. For some unknown reason, they had decided they didn't want him any more, at four years old, and sent him to Labrador Rescue. Harry Cook, who runs the service, assured me he had a lovely home and I could visit him anytime.

All my puppies are sold on the understanding that if at any time the owners don't want their dog, it is returned to me immediately. Why hadn't these people done this? Why had they just abandoned that poor dog at the age of four? Probably they were ashamed of themselves and couldn't face me.

The next call was from an owner of one of Mocha's puppies, now five months old. The puppy had problems. First of all, she appeared to have difficulty in house-training, and left little puddles here and there. The owner's vet had treated the puppy for cystitis over the last couple of months, with no success. I had managed to persuade the owner to take the puppy to my vet and it was then discovered that one of the tubes inside had not grown to the correct length and the poor little thing could not control her waterworks. My vet assured the owner that this would correct itself as the puppy grew.

I had done everything I could to help: I'd paid the vet's bills and promised to return the amount she had paid me for the puppy. I didn't want to be responsible for selling a defective puppy, despite the fact that it was not my fault, for I had no knowledge of this defect and it is not hereditary. But, the big snag was I didn't have any money! I have never been able to make any money from breeding dogs. The cost of feeding and heating them alone is phenomenal. Consequently, I had offered to pay the owner back over the next few months. She was now screaming at me on the other end of the phone. She wasn't prepared to wait and unless I refunded her money immediately, a solicitor's letter would follow. I replaced the receiver and sobbed, in total despair.

CHAPTER FIFTEEN

NEVER SAY NEVER AGAIN

Not being able to breed Labradors any more, I told myself constantly, wasn't the end of the world. After all, I had Katy to train and now Psyche. I was determined to approach the training and my shows with renewed vigour. It would take my mind off all my problems, and everyone needs an outlet. But that wasn't to be. As if life hadn't had enough by knocking me over, it then decided to trample on me. Katy began to limp on her front left leg and I was back in that vet's waiting room. I'm not sure which I hate most, going to the bank or the vet's. They both make me feel sick with nerves. A vet's waiting room is even worse than the doctor's. Everyone sits, nervous, twiddling at their dogs' leads or clutching cat baskets and the atmosphere seems charged with foreboding. On that particular day, I was oblivious to all those other owners. I remembered losing Shadow, and that began with her limping on her front left leg.

I sat, stiff with sheer terror. It wasn't possible, I told myself, that Katy could have bone cancer. That couldn't happen to me twice. Katy was X-rayed and, much to my relief, the X-ray showed a small chip of bone had been pulled off the elbow joint. Rest, I was told. Six weeks and she'll be fine.

After the six weeks, I took Katy for a short walk and she limped, but this time on the right leg. Sadly, there's no National Health Service for pets and any money I could get hold of was just being gobbled up by the vet. Her right shoulder was now X-rayed, to show that it was full of arthritis. Another dream shattered. I had worked, over the last five years, with Katy, to achieve my dream of being eligible for the top class in obedience but the exercises required in Test C would aggravate Katy's shoulder condition. I had no option but to retire her.

I decided not to sit and sob about it because it gives me a headache. I wouldn't let life get me down. I'd put all my energies into training Psyche. It was February when Psyche came into season, at long last, at the age of sixteen months. I couldn't wait to have her spayed and get that all behind me. Most vets won't spay a bitch until they have had their first season, and the recommended time is three months after it. I put a note in my diary that Psyche would be due for spaying about the end of April and I'd have Katy done at the same time.

The gales in February blew everything down, including our back fence, but I consoled myself with the knowledge that the dogs couldn't get out. Between them and the back fence was a lawn and a smaller fence, to prevent the dogs ruining the bit of grass we had left. It was impossible to repair it at the time, for the ground was frozen solid. All of February and March I was chafing at the bit, waiting for the weather to ease up so that I could take Psyche out on the park and train her up for the show season that began in April. Psyche appeared very sluggish on her training. At first, I thought it may be her winter lay-off, but then I began to wonder.

It was early one morning when I had to face the truth. I was sitting in the kitchen, still bleary-eyed, on my third cup of tea, when I noticed Psyche's shape. She had always been so long and slender, but now she looked . . . fat! That was impossible, I told myself. I began to run my hands along her body and round her tummy. It was solid and hard.

"What have you been doing, Psyche?" I asked her. I was greeted by the whole body giggle and the lick on the nose. "Have you been eating something in the night?" I watched her very carefully that day, hoping that the tummy swelling would go down. It didn't. Over tea I discussed it with Don.

"Maybe," I said, cheerfully, "she's having a false pregnancy."

"Yes, of course she is. I don't know what you're worried about. She doesn't look ill or anything, does she?"

I had to agree. She looked very healthy. Her coat gleamed far more than usual. As the days passed by, Psyche grew larger and I had to face the fact that the pregnancy was definitely not false. I knew who the father was. A collie called Ben lived three doors down from us and once or twice I'd seen him leaving through the fallen fence at the back of the garden but, for the life of me, I couldn't work out how he'd had the opportunity to mate Psyche.

I needed another litter like I needed a visit from the VAT man, and a mongrel litter at that. Not that I've anything against mongrels. It was the cost of feeding them that frightened me. There was no way I could recoup my money on a cross-bred litter. And there was another worry to be considered: when would they be due? On a controlled mating, the date could be worked out easily. I had no idea when Ben had his wicked way with Psyche. I just had to guess that it would be somewhere between the twentieth and the thirtieth of April. Meanwhile Psyche grew to such enormous proportions, I was afraid she'd go *bang*!

Waiting for Psyche's litter to be born seemed the darkest hour in my life. An unwanted litter on the way — how would I find them homes? — how would I pay for the enormous quantity of food I knew they would eat? I had no prospects of a job, no money. Like a hand from heaven, something wonderful began to happen in my mind.

Over the last few years, I'd been trying to write children's books. They'd never worked. They always turned out wrong and I ended up scrapping them and throwing them in the bin. But as I paced around, waiting for Psyche's puppies to be born, a picture materialized in my imagination of a dog and a girl. The dog was mainly black, with a brilliant white patch on his chest. He was a little fluffier than a Labrador, with a long, pointed face and very dark, brown eyes that shone with wisdom. The picture of this dog in my mind became an obsession and, without really knowing what I was doing, I fetched the tape recorder. It normally takes me about six months to write a book, organizing plots and characters, setting each chapter out. The book I was to write then took me a day and a half. When I switched the tape recorder on, I had no idea what I was going to say, except for, "This is chapter one, page one. . . ."

It was as if I was taking part in a dream that I had no control over. I wasn't making up the story. It's as if I was the translator. The words and chapters flew into my mind. The dog I had pictured was called Shep and he befriended a girl with a visual handicap. When Don came in to see where his morning cup of coffee had got to, I was amazed at the time and the fact that I had already reached chapter six.

"What are you doing?" Don asked me.

I told him I was writing a children's book.

"You didn't tell me you had one in mind."

"I didn't," I confessed. "It's very strange."

"Tell me about it."

I quickly went through the story so far and he asked me what happened next. To my horror, I didn't know. I felt a little afraid . . . out of control. Something very strange was happening to me, but I was compelled to write the book. I had to drag myself away from the tape recorder to cook Don's lunch and then to feed the dogs. I was mentally shattered that night when I fell into bed, but determined to be up early the next morning to continue the book. It seemed to be a force beyond my control driving me. I must state here that I have never been particularly religious, more practical and logical. In fact, after my successful eye operation, I remember many people approaching me saying, "You should thank God for your sight." I thanked Mr Shearing for his skill. Logically, I told myself, if I was to thank God for giving me my sight, why should I not blame him for taking it away in the first place? And, if there was a God, how could he be so callous as to sit up there and watch the world in its terrible turmoil, to let many thousands of children die of starvation, to see humans suffer the tormented death of cancer, or the handicap of spina bifida. As a child, I had said my prayers and thought of God as a father figure, someone to rely on in times of need, but, like many people, my childish faith had been slowly eroded away with adult life.

The incident that finally convinced me there was no God was actually the birth of a litter of puppies. It had been a few years back, when Buttons had given birth to nine puppies and I was marvelling at the miracle of life. God created them, I thought, but I have to look after them, love them and feed them and care for them and ensure that their homes were perfect. Not only that, but to continue caring for their welfare long after they had been sold to their new homes. I was a sort of God to those puppies, the giver of life. If I cared so much what happened to those dogs through their life, why didn't God care for his creatures? That was the point when I became an atheist. And now I had written this book called *Shep*, and it gave me all the answers to those religious questions we all ask.

I was amazed that this type of book should come from my imagination. I still can't believe it. I don't really know what I believe now. I would like to believe that the idea for the book did come from somewhere else, but maybe that's being a little egotistical. But, whatever the answer is, it changed my whole outlook on life. The most important thing is love and I am lucky: I have Don and Kerensa and all the dogs to love. And then there's sight. No-one can take those things away from me, not the VAT man or the taxman or the bank manager.

Three days after completing *Shep*, Psyche's puppies were born. After five, I told her that was enough, more than enough to find homes for. When the eighth puppy came, I begged her not to have any more. I could see my feeding costs rising by the minute. She didn't stop until there were ten little puppies around her and there, amongst them, was a black fluffy one, with a brilliant white chest!

CHAPTER SIXTEEN

SERENDIPITY

In all the litters I've bred, there's never been a special puppy that I have fallen in love with. On the contrary, I've tried to love them all and give each one individual attention without losing my heart to any of them. This litter was different. From the moment the little puppy who looked like my description of Shep was born, I fell for him — hook, line and sinker.

Even in the early days of their growth, Shep appeared so very different from the others. He was the largest and the fluffiest puppy, and he had charisma. At just over a fortnight old, he alone was reacting to my voice, trying to sit up and paw the air with his front legs. I found that totally irresistible. As hard as I tried, I couldn't prevent myself from picking him up every time and cuddling him. Both Don and Kerensa were amazed that this one little puppy should look just like the dog I had described and they, too, were attracted to him. From the very day of his birth, Kerensa begged me to keep him.

"Don't be silly," I said. "We've got six dogs. That's far too many. Seven would be total lunacy!"

I sat with Psyche and her litter in the puppy house hour after hour, just watching "my boy". He was developing much quicker than his brothers and sisters, being the first to bark and the first to climb out of the box days before the others were interested in the outside world. I desperately tried to turn my attention to the other puppies, but it was no use. He was the one I couldn't resist picking up and loving first. He would reward me by gently patting me on the end of the nose with a front paw. I told him, over and over again, that there was no way I could keep seven dogs. I shed a tear over his lovely black head nearly every day at the thought that I would have to part with him.

As a whole, I found the litter far more fascinating than one of pure-bred Labradors. Labrador puppies are so predictable. At three weeks, they will begin to associate sounds. Between three and four weeks, they begin to look and register visual images. At five weeks, they are all climbing out of their box and galloping about and at six weeks they are little monsters. But Psyche's cross-bred puppies were very different. They all developed at different times. My boy being first to do everything, of course. At four weeks old, they were actually barking at me when I entered the puppy house and had certainly started practising their guard-dog bit at an early age. And each one was very different to look at. Some had soft, silky coats. Others were fluffy and thick-coated. Nearly all of them had a white splash or mark on the chest, and they were far more demanding than a litter of Labradors, begging me to play with them or nurse them late into the night.

For six weeks, I lived in terror and anguish at the thought that my puppy would have to go . . . and would I be able to find ten homes for cross-bred puppies? I soon discovered that people were clamouring for "colliadors". Prospective owners travelled from far and wide to own one of Psyche's "mistakes".

Without exception, every single person chose "my" boy. He was the one puppy who waltzed out of the bed, tail high, with great confidence, and introduced himself to everyone.

Logically, he had to go. I couldn't afford to feed seven dogs and we certainly didn't have acres of ground to run them in, but I just could not say yes. I made excuses. "He wouldn't suit you," I told them. "He's too dominant" . . . "Oh, he's going to be much too big for you."

I reeled off all kinds of excuses to the people who wanted "my" little puppy and convinced them that one of the other puppies would be much more suited to their way of life. Many of them turned away when I told them they couldn't have my puppy.

Every day when Kerensa came home from school, she ran up to the puppy house, calling, "Has he gone? Has someone fetched him?"

Sheepishly, I would tell her no, that I hadn't found a suitable home for him yet. It was Don who solved my terrible dilemma. He could no longer stand by and watch me suffer. Without saying a word, he marched purposefully up to the puppy house, picked my little boy out and brought him into the kitchen. He placed him gently down in the middle of the floor.

"That's it," he told me. "We're keeping him."

"But how?" I stammered.

"No buts . . . he's staying!"

I felt as if someone had just taken a clamp off my heart. I realized that there was no way I could have parted with him. It was just impossible, he had to stay with us. But I had to face the problem of money, and food, and looking after seven dogs.

"There is just one proviso." Don grinned at me.

"What's that?" I asked, expecting him to say that I'd got to get a morning cleaning job to feed them.

"I name this one. I'm not having you lumbering me with any more names like 'Psyche'."

I had chosen Psyche's name a long time before she was born. I've always loved that name for a dog. Most people think it's awful. It's stayed with me from my childhood days, in the 'fifties, when every Sunday the family would sit round the radio and listen to *Life of Bliss*, with George Cole. There was a pet fox terrier in that programme called Psyche. Don had objected fervently.

"I'm not walking round the woods every morning shouting *that* name." But he did.

"We're going to call him Pip!"

That got lengthened by me to "Pipsqueak", because he did — squeak, that is, for whatever he wanted.

I knew, from the temperament tests I'd done with the litter, that he was a very dominant male — something, I thought, that wouldn't suit me. And then there was Bracken. I had the misconceived idea that two males would not agree, especially when they were sharing their home with bitches. I have always preferred bitches. Believing that Bracken was the exception, I thought males were difficult to train, always roaming after the bitches and lacking in affection for human beings. Pipsqueak was going to prove to me that I was very wrong. So was Bracken, who loved Pip from the moment he set paw in the house. Maybe he was relieved to have another male around.

I soon discovered that my temperament tests were right. Pip was very dominant. At eight weeks old, he would growl at me when I approached him to investigate his bulging, black jaws. Just like the Labrador puppies, he was always finding something nice to chew. It's very tempting to laugh at a tiny puppy trying to stand his ground, growling, especially when he's got a pair of your tights hanging out the side of his jaws, but I knew I had to be firm right from the beginning. I took hold of the scruff of his neck and told him I wouldn't accept that type of behaviour. Prising the tights out of his mouth, I would swop it for a titbit. It took about two weeks to cure Pip of this aggression and I often wonder what would have happened if he'd gone to a less knowledgeable home.

I thought the Labrador puppies were quick, intelligent and mischievous. Pip made them look like amateurs. While the Labradors were sitting around, contemplating the world, Pip would be in, steal their precious squeaky toy and run round the garden three times before any of them noticed it was missing. He was quick to learn, too. Only once did he get his head stuck in the wrought-iron gate!

There were times when he showed such intelligence and perception, he made me feel inferior. The Labradors sleep most of the day, or potter about the place, showing mild interest in what's happening around them. Pip watches. He watches everything. While I'm in the kitchen preparing the dinner, he watches me peel the potatoes. He takes great interest as I fetch the pans from the cupboard. He appears to take a mental note of where the plates and knives and forks come from. Wherever I am and whatever I'm doing, Pip's eyes are following me.

He has the ability to put across his needs to me by just looking, with eyes that are so dark brown they are almost black. When I look into those dark brown eyes, I see pools of love and understanding and, although I state categorically I am not a "soppy" dog lover, I am sure Pip knows exactly what I am thinking, and he certainly has the ability to let me know what he's thinking.

He may be just "an accident", but what a happy one! Hence, his official registered name, for show purposes, is Serendipity, which means "happy accident".

CHAPTER SEVENTEEN

PIP'S PROGRESS

———————————

Pip was incredibly easy to train, his reactions being so much faster than the Labradors'. On the park, he responds to a recall instantly. Even when he is galloping after another dog, he'll turn on a sixpence. I think that he has a far better memory than the Labradors too. He appears to retain his training and even to anticipate it.

Every morning, Don takes the dogs round the woods for an hour's walk. Like everything else in a household with seven dogs, routine must be the by-word. I let them out of the dog room one by one. Every morning, I have to tell the Labradors to sit and wait, but as soon as I approach the dog room door, Pip sits instantly and won't offer to move until his name is called.

Perhaps it's having Pip that makes Mocha look even more dilatory. Whenever she's let out of the dog room, she leaps about in sheer excitement, but forgets what's happening. She looks at me, her ears lolloping up and down, as if to say, Gosh, something terribly exciting is about to happen, but what is it?

I steer her to the hall. "Mocha, in the car!"

She jumps down the hall like a spring lamb and, at the front door, turns and looks at me again. This is so wonderful, but what am I supposed to do?

I open the front door, reminding her that it's walk time. She always falls down the step and then turns to look at it, as if to say, I'm sure that step wasn't here yesterday.

"In the car, Mocha, for your walk," I need to remind her half a dozen times.

On the whole, our canine population is ageing. Buttons is ten and has greyed around the muzzle. Buttons has always been ungainly and she lumbers down the hall like a hippopotamus. Bracken is nine and he, too, is getting grey whiskers. Teak and Mocha are eight. Although Teak still hares about the park with youthful exuberance, her waistline is a little thicker than it was. Katy, poor little Katy, is only five, but her arthritic shoulder has slowed her down. Psyche and Pip are now the youthful members of the household.

I am sure it is having young dogs around the place that keeps me going. Most other women of my age seem terribly unfit, pale and slow. I don't see many other forty-year-old women running and leaping about the park as I do. No wonder I get strange looks, but there's no way I want to grow old gracefully.

As Pip grew, the collie side of his temperament became much more apparent — speed, willingness to learn and a protective instinct. While it's very pleasing to have a dog who will protect me against all comers, it can be very dangerous unless it's controlled correctly. Pip would take exception to any male adults or youths that came near me in the park, racing round them in circles and barking. This is the exact procedure used by police dogs to stop and hold a criminal — to keep far enough away from them to be out of boot's reach and to circle fast enough to stop the criminal making a getaway. Pip would have won first-class honours in any police dog trial. Except these poor unsuspecting walkers were hardly hardened criminals.

I soon cured this unpleasant habit by calling Pip in and making him do a "down-stay" until the walker had passed. I have tried not to curb this protective instinct completely. I let him give strange looking people a bark or two before telling him "that will do!" It's a reassuring feeling to have a dog who will protect me, in this day and age. His attitude is the same to callers at the house. The Labradors all dive in and try and wash the caller to death. Pip stands back, reserving judgement, and won't let a stranger touch him until he feels sure he's safe.

I am painting a very rosy picture of my "colliador" and I must admit that the collie side of his nature is a very attractive one to me, but I can see from Pip's active brain that a collie wouldn't be easy to live with and would need lots of exercise and work. Pip is often far too intelligent for his own good, like being able to open the back door. The Labradors have tried getting in the back door at feeding time for years, but they've never succeeded. Pip came along and showed them how to do it. All he had to do was to put his paw on the handle and depress it and the door opened. Pip is smart enough to know that, once he's opened the back door, he's not allowed in. He sits on the doorstep and grins as the Labradors rush into the kitchen, only to be turned back out again.

When the Labradors take to their bed after their dinner, Pip paces the floor, wondering what he can do next. If I ignore his pleas for entertainment, he stares at me. I can often feel those eyes, even on my back. In fact, many of my friends have told me he gives them the jitters when he looks at them. One of them said she felt as if he was looking into her soul. If I ignore that burning stare, he comes out with the squeaks and then he'll throw something at me — literally. He'll find a toy, or anything he wants to play with and instead of bringing it and dropping it at my feet, he stands in front of me and gives a quick flick of the head, hurling his toy at me. Then he dances. For a big dog, he's incredibly light on his feet. The Labradors tend to plod and lumber. He skips over the ground.

I have discovered, to my cost, that he's a very unpredictable dog. The Labradors will walk on a loose lead, regardless of bangs, cats shooting across in front of them, children on skateboards and so on. They seem oblivious to their surroundings. Pip walks on tiptoe, his ears held out to the side of his head, his nose always testing the air, always on the alert. The other day, a little girl came out of her gate wearing her mum's high-heeled shoes. Pip almost had hysterics, bucking and rearing up in the air like a wild stallion. But, of course, this is his sensitivity and it is extremely useful in his training.

Once I'd learned how sensitive he was, I was able to train him much quicker. For instance, the Labradors are not sensitive to my body movements. Whatever I do with shoulders or hands, when we are working together, they ignore. They only work on verbal commands. Pip watches my body movements. For a long time, when I was training him to do heel work, I couldn't understand why sometimes he jumped back on me and then I realized a twitch of the left shoulder meant, to him, a left turn and he was jumping back out of the way.

He can read my body language better than I can and he knows when I am annoyed with him before I have said a word. I often wonder whether dogs put an act on of apology. Bracken always puts his rose-petal ears on and drags his back legs if he thinks I'm annoyed with him. Katy will hide. Psyche freezes and turns into a solid block of stone until the crisis is over. Pipsqueak throws himself on the floor, his head down, but I know it's not for real that he's looking submissive and guilty for the instant I show any sign of forgiveness, he leaps up, trying to paw at my nose. In a six-week-old puppy, that was endearing but having enormous paws pat the end of your nose can be dangerous.

Labradors have always been my first love, obviously because of Emma. She was very intelligent, quick witted and smart, and I thought all Labradors were like that. Naturally, I've always tried to find another Emma. This is part of my problem — it's why we have so many dogs around us. While I can see some of Emma's assets in each of my Labradors, they are so different from her. She could remember things. Routes that we took only once, she would retain for years. Her reactions to difficult situations in the street were instant and positive and, up to the age of fourteen, she could outwalk almost any dog. The five Labradors I own now fall far short of Emma's virtues. Over the years, I have managed to seal a very close relationship with each of them, but nothing special. With Pip, I can feel a magic developing between us, an unspoken understanding, just like Emma. I only need to show him something once and he remembers. Maybe it's the Shep story that's brought us closer together, but whatever it is, Pip brought with him more than a magic kind of relationship.

CHAPTER EIGHTEEN

THE LIGHT DAWNS

I didn't want to get a job in an office, but I would have worked anywhere to get myself out of the dreadful financial situation I was in. To be truthful, the thought of working on a switchboard again made me shudder. To be shut away from the sunlight and the birds, not to be able to walk with the dogs on the park in the daytime would be like imprisonment to me. With an extra dog mouth to feed, I was even more desperate for money and maybe it was turning forty that cleared my brain, or maybe it was the coming of Pip. I don't know, but, suddenly, I seemed to know what I should do and how to earn the money I so desperately needed.

I had the capability and the knowledge to write a pets column for newspapers or magazines. I set about this new idea with great enthusiasm. I photostated hundreds of typed letters and sent them out to every newspaper and magazine I could find in the *Writers' and Artists' Yearbook*. At first, I received only negative answers and was beginning to doubt my capabilities again, but I knew that this was the answer. So I posted yet more letters into our local box and, at last, I received a "yes please" from our local evening paper, the *Nottingham Evening Post*, to produce a weekly article on pets.

It's very strange that when you are down and getting nowhere, nothing good happens. Once the turn comes, there is only one way and that's up. The "ups" in my life I now refer to as "Pip's Law".

For *two* women's magazines then wanted my column! I chose to write for *My Weekly*. These two posts threw me into a whole new way of life. I could answer any questions on dogs and cats and write about them till the cows came home, but there were many other pets I had to research into. I visited pet shops and pony rescue organizations, and aquariums and animal farms of all types.

I've enjoyed most of my assignments. The one I least enjoyed was going to visit "Handsome". He was a teacher's pet . . . a gigantic tarantula. I entered the classroom, pen and paper clutched in a shaking hand. The children were very excited about showing their pet off to a newspaper reporter (for that's what I had become). I tried, for their sake, not to show any fear when I saw a couple of furry legs clutching their way out of the cage, and I backed off towards the door in terror. I wasn't fooling the children — they all knew I was scared to death. They, on the other hand, were clamouring to hold this revolting creature. The spider ran up their arms, across their faces and down their necks and they giggled with joy. The teacher assured me that tarantulas were not poisonous and I was welcome to hold him. I muttered something about not getting paid danger money and another appointment I was late for already. After asking a few hasty questions, I beat a retreat to the safety of my dogs.

I soon discovered I had to keep a very tight check on myself when visiting other people's pets. My natural instinct to love anything four-legged and furry did, I'm afraid, lead me to bring home more pets. Fortunately — or unfortunately, whichever way you look at it — my lack of money and space prevented me from offering house or garden room to the larger ones. Given a free rein, I would turn our back garden into *The Good Life*, with chickens and goats and a sheep or two. Sadly, the suburban area in which we live doesn't permit that type of pet. I still don't understand why. I'd much rather wake up to the sound of a cockerel than that of motorbikes haring up the main road.

I did bring some quiet, small pets home: our two chinchillas. Until I visited a local chinchilla ranch to write about it for one of the pets columns, I had no idea these creatures had become so popular as pets. They're delightful little things, looking like a cross between a squirrel and a rabbit. Originally they were imported and bred over here for their pelts, but they are much prettier alive than dead. They have gained their popularity because they can live either inside or out, in a metal cage. They are very clean, there is no smell and they don't make a noise — so they are ideal pets for the flat-dweller. They also have a long life-span, twenty years being their average age. They are naturally shy little creatures. That, in itself, was a challenge to me to tame them.

Chilli, the male, is a beautiful soft beige colour. Carne, the female, is white overlaid with a pink sheen. They are fascinating to watch, as they use their front paws like squirrels. At least these two little chinchillas have given me the opportunity to breed something. I love looking after baby animals. There's something exciting about breeding, expecting litters and watching their development.

I have explained how I have been forced to give up breeding the dogs and now only Rahni remains of the cats. She's twelve, and a crotchety old thing. I have loved all my Siamese in different ways, but Ming held something very special. She was a true Siamese, friendly, outgoing and very mischievous. She would race across the mantelshelf, breaking every china model on the way, hurl up the curtains to the pelmet, down again and steal a piece of food from the end of my fork before it quite reached my mouth. But, more than that, I associated Ming with Emma. They had been virtually brought up together and they were the best of friends. It was Ming who would steal food for Emma. She would jump on the kitchen worktops and bat morsels of food into Emma's ever-open jaws.

I vowed that I would never have any more Siamese when I lost Ming. I couldn't face the heartache. Ming had produced beautiful kittens, but two of her last litter were born with cleft palates. Surgically, nothing can be done to correct this hereditary defect and I knew these kittens would die. Despite that, I hand-fed them for as long as I could. Totally irrational. I should have taken them directly to the vet to have them put down, but life is so precious for me and I always hoped and prayed that I could rear the defective kittens.

Many breeders get hardened to their losses. I can't. I get weakened every time and feel, on the loss of each animal, that part of my body has gone with them. I fervently hope I never lose any of the chinchilla babies.

Kerensa is always begging me for a kitten of her very own. She was heart-broken at the loss of her lovely Holly, but so far I've managed to resist, telling Kerensa that while we have Rahni it would be very unfair to bring another cat into the house. Kerensa and Rahni don't see eye to eye. To put it bluntly, every time Kerensa approaches Rahni, Rahni spits at her. Not that she would do her any damage . . . Rahni is frightened of her own shadow, and I'm the only person that she will actually walk up to — if she feels in the mood.

I managed to sidetrack Kerensa's longing for a cat by offering her two goldfish and a beautiful hamster called Crystal. Kerensa had begged me for a hamster for three years. Eventually I relented and when I saw Crystal, I was hooked. She was the most beautiful looking creature, a long-coated silver. Kerensa worshipped her from the moment she set eyes on her and tended her with great care and gentleness. Every morning at breakfast, I was treated to what Crystal had done during the night.

"She went on her wheel," Kerensa would tell me, "and then up to her bed. She chewed on the bars for a while . . ." And so it went on. I'm sure Kerensa could write a manual on hamster behaviour.

One awful morning, Kerensa came downstairs screaming.

"Crystal's gone! She's got out of her cage. She'll die!" she wailed. "I know she will!"

I tried not to panic.

"If she gets under the floorboards, she'll freeze to death!"

For the next three days and nights we searched. I took every clothes drawer out in the house and searched it thoroughly. We moved all the beds, mattresses, blankets, sheets. Wardrobes were shoved to one side. Carpets were rolled up. We searched every inch of every room in the house, but Crystal was nowhere to be found. We all went through such agonies, picturing our little Crystal trapped, starving and cold. Every night, Kerensa set a type of food trap, in case Crystal returned while she was asleep. It was a box balanced by a pencil over a bowl of food. I hated to tell Kerensa that I was sure her idea would never work, even if Crystal did come back in the night. But I was wrong. At four o'clock in the morning, Kerensa was shaking me.

"Crystal's come back! Quick! Come and have a look! I caught her in the box."

The hamster was back, starving and thirsty, but a bowl of food and water and a good sleep returned her to her pretty self the next day. We never did discover where she'd been, or how she managed to get out of the cage. The whole incident really made me appreciate Kerensa, for she loves animals just as much as I do. In fact, she wants to be a vet. I hope she succeeds. It will save me a fortune in vet's bills!

I've always had a secret fear that Kerensa may grow up to hate animals. I've often met people who've been turned against pets because their parents kept them and lavished all their affection on them. Now I have no fears in this direction. I must have caught the right balance between child and pets.

"Where are you off to?" Don asked me one day as he came in for his morning coffee.

"I'm going to look at a herd of goats."

He groaned and reached in the cupboard for the coffee jar.

"Wouldn't it be nice to have a goat? It would keep the lawn short and we could milk it every morning."

He mumbled something into the milk pan. I was deliberately teasing him. "Don't they eat fences and flowers as well?" he asked me.

"Well, you could build a big brick wall round the back garden . . . and think of the time it would save you in mowing!"

He said nothing as he heaped the sugar into his coffee mug, a worried look on his face. I'm not sure whether he thought I was going to bring a goat home, or whether he was working out how high to build the brick wall, but I couldn't tease him any longer. I began to giggle. He breathed a sigh of relief. I have managed to stave off the urge to bring anything else home. Common sense must be winning at last.

I realized that writing pets columns would take a lot of time, researching and visiting. What I hadn't bargained for were the letters. They poured in by the sackload, with every problem for me to solve, from an over-sexed tortoise to a budgie with an enlarged beak. I had become the pets' answer to an agony aunt.

My confidence was returning in great waves and I realized I could offer a great deal of help in the way of dog training. My pet classes boomed, so much so that the local authority employed me to take their dog training classes. I love teaching people, for that's what it's all about. I could train the dogs, but the art is showing the owners how to do it. I confess that dog training in pet classes gives a very one-sided view of the canine population. Because I get all the problem dogs, I often return home from a training lesson in despair. Don always knows what's happened.

"Did you have another difficult owner?" he asks.

"Oh yes, the dog is beautiful, but I can't do anything with the human!"

I do get a lot of really beautiful dogs with difficult owners, but what worries me most of all are the aggressive dogs. When there are children in a family with a large, aggressive dog, I have nightmares. There's nothing I can do about it because, more often than not, the owners are totally incapable of gaining control. Dogs, although they may have been domesticated for thousands of years, are still pack animals and have the inborn instinct to lead or follow. A leader dog will want to dominate his flock, be it other dogs, adults or children. But trying to convince these owners that they must take definite action to put their dog in its place is like beating my head against a brick wall, and sometimes I want to give it all up and lead an easy life. But I can't. It's like a driving force, a need to get out there and help people.

My fortune has turned. In fact, I hardly have a minute to call my own. Mornings are taken up with writing, the afternoons with housework, and evenings with dog training. I often have to forego my lunch or tea-break to make time to train my own dogs. But it's worth it, for going to shows is a real pleasure to me, especially now that my confidence is travelling down through the lead to the dogs. And Psyche has now won three Firsts and moved up the obedience classes. Pipsqueak's training is a joy, because he's so easy and willing.

When Psyche works, she's thorough, reliable and method-ical. Pip is entirely different. He works with style, exuding charisma, but he is unpredictable. I discovered that as soon as I began to enter him for the shows. His first round was absolute perfection, except that when he went to retrieve the dumbbell he lay down on it instead of picking it up and bringing it back to me. With ears held back, he stared at me with those deep brown eyes. I couldn't fathom what was going on in that little brain of his, but after a verbal reminder, he picked it up and rushed back to me. I've never worried about the "stay" exercises at shows. Labradors are so idle, they stay anywhere. But not Pipsqueak. I was astonished, on my first stay exercise, when I left him with confidence and walked out of the ring, only to discover that Pip had walked out with me. He immediately realized his mistake, reared up on hind legs, touched my face with his paws and then lay down on the floor.

Pip is like a large, expensive diamond. Whenever you look into it, you are fascinated by the different colours and facets it shows you. I wonder if he will ever calm down and be "ploddy" like the Labradors, for, at the moment, he is incredibly active and wants me to play with him constantly. I purchased a new rubber toy for him the other day. On the packet, it promised to amuse bored dogs: "Dogs will play with this for hours." What it should have said on the packet was: "For owners who have time on their hands," for Pip won't play with this toy unless I share the games. Katy and Psyche would like to play with him but he won't have that. He guards his rubber toy against the other dogs then throws it into my lap and demands I play with him.

I feel very sorry for people who can't or don't have pets, for the happiness that our pets have brought us is immeasurable and I could wish for no more out of life. I have to face the fact that I will never own a boarding kennels — not unless I win the football pools! I could, so easily, have obtained that life-long dream if only I'd been careful and saved my money. But I let the opportunity slip away, like sand slipping through fingers. I have no-one to blame but myself. I have made my mistakes — I hope I've learned by them — and, in all honesty, could I ask for more out of one lifetime? I can see. Don and I are still very much in love. We have Kerensa, a perfectly sighted daughter. And our pets!